Satan's Strategy to Torment through Physical Ambush

Satan's Strategy to Torment through Physical Ambush

Educating God's Soldiers of Satan's Plot to Shatter Faith through Sickness and Disease

R. C. JETTE

RESOURCE *Publications* · Eugene, Oregon

Resource Publications
An Imprint of Wipf and Stock Publishers
199 W. 8th Ave., Suite 3
Eugene, OR 97401

www.wipfandstock.com

PAPERBACK ISBN: 978-1-5326-8636-8
HARDCOVER ISBN: 978-1-5326-8637-5
EBOOK ISBN: 978-1-5326-8638-2

Manufactured in the U.S.A.   MAY 1, 2019

All Scriptures are taken from the King James Version (KJV), public domain.

This book is dedicated to my Lord Jesus Christ! To Him I give all thanks and praise.

Also, I dedicate it to my husband Paul, and my granddaughter, Sarah Elizabeth who I will join when my journey here is over.

I give special thanks to Wipf and Stock Publishers for making it all possible, for their professional staff who worked patiently with me, and for their continued encouragement. They have caused my heart to be overwhelmed with thanksgiving to the Lord for them.

Previously published by them:

Storms Are Faith's Workout: Preparing Christians for Spiritual Ambush (2018), *The Elfdins and the Gold Temple: An Oralee Chronicle* (2018), *Charlie McGee and the Leprechaun: Life's Curious Twist of Events* (2019), *Faith's Journey Confronts Obstacles: Instructing God's Soldiers to Overcome in His Armor* (2019), and *Spiritual Shipwreck on the Horizon: Exhorting Christians to Contend for the Faith and Comprehend the Deceitfulness of Sin* (2019)

But he was wounded for our transgressions, he was bruised for our iniquities: the chastisement of our peace was upon him; and with his stripes we are healed.

—Isaiah 53:5

CONTENTS

Introduction

I MENTIONED IN MY first book, *Storms Are Faith's Workout: Preparing Christians for Spiritual Ambush* about the thesis for my master's degree. At the time, I didn't have any intention of using it as a foundation for another book, nor did I have any conception of writing my second book on faith, *Faith's Journey Confronts Obstacles: Instructing God's Soldiers to Overcome in His Armor*. It was about half way through Faith's Journey that I knew that I was going to do this third book on faith.

The Lord revealed that I had to lay the groundwork with the other two books before this could be written. Although this book springs from my thesis, it is only a foundation on which to establish another truth concerning faith. The intention of *Satan's Strategy to Torment Through Physical Ambush: Educating God's Soldiers of Satan's Plot to Shatter Faith Through Sickness and Disease* is to build upon my other books about faith and to further educate God's soldiers concerning Satan and his diabolical strategies to hinder our faith journey.

This book is more scholastic in its content than the other two books in that I will quote other theologians and ministers to bring forth the evidence that I believe is needed. I am convinced that this book will enlighten many of God's soldiers regarding the physical battle that they are fighting at present. Ignorance is a flaw in God's people and the devil uses it to convince us to believe his lies. In the middle of a storm or when facing an incredible obstacle, we tend to forget that the devil is a liar and there is no truth in him (John 8:44).

God is aware of Satan's strategy, as he has given him permission. We saw that the devil cannot do anything to God's child without permission from God in my first book. This book will bring it to a personal level and with the information from the two previous books, God's soldiers will learn how to be victorious and overcome by faith any and all of Satan's stratagems.

It is my opinion that this book is what is needed today, for I have confronted the obstacle of being physically ambushed by Satan to afflict me though bodily ailments. Only as we are aware of his devices can we know how to stand against them. As God's soldiers put on the whole armor of God, we will recognize the enemy's strategy to afflict us physically.

If you haven't read my previous two books concerning faith, I recommend that you do. They will give you a foundation of faith to help prepare you for this book. Only as we are aware of Satan's strategies can we understand what is happening in our life. Unlike Job, who will be discussed in chapter five, God's soldiers can know how to overcome the storm assailing their physical body. Only as we comprehend that the devil does not have authority over us, but it is God's soldiers that have the authority over all the power of the enemy, will we stand in God's armor and overcome (Luke 10:19).

God has impressed upon my heart that His soldiers are settling for less than what He has promised in His word. Many lack a knowledge of Scripture. Some have been taught wrong doctrine and are ignorant of what God has pledged in His word. All of the promises belong to His children, and it is up us to know and stand upon them. This book is to help us understand that it is God's will that we recognize what the devil is doing and to overcome his lies by faith.

Christian, you have picked up this book because you are struggling physically. You have read about the healings in the Bible, but healing seems to have alluded you. It is my prayer that you will understand that healing belongs to you as God's child, for it is the children's bread (Matthew 15:26). When Jesus told the woman of Canaan that, He was referring to the healing that she desired for her daughter. Please understand that Jesus made unequivocally clear that healing belongs to God's soldiers. As long as you know that God is not calling you home, it is His will for you to be in health. That's what this book proposes to communicate. It is meant to reveal to you what the will of God is concerning your health. Read it through to the end and you will come away with the knowledge needed to confront by faith Satan and his lies about healing!

I

The Acceptance of Sickness in God's Soldiers

> And he shall speak great words against the most High,
> and shall wear out the saints of the most High, and think
> to change times and laws: and they shall be given into
> his hand until a time and times and the dividing of time
> (Daniel 7:25).

THE SUBJECT OF THIS book is to establish that Satan plans to mentally afflict the saints through sickness and disease as cited in Daniel 7:25. Since he has been granted permission (given into his hands), he will use every diabolical malady conceivable against their physical bodies. This will be done through deception (Genesis 3:4–5). As he deceived Eve's conviction in the word of God, he will similarly splinter the faith of many.[1] Satan's motive is to cause doubt in what God says about sickness and disease. The devil is the father of lies (John 8:44), and he is using his deceptive ambushes to take God's soldiers off balance. When we are unbalanced, we can sometimes be swayed to believe what is not true or what is contrary to God's word. That is when the devil has us in a compromising position if we are not clothed in the full armor of God.

1. Stamps, *The Full Life Study Bible*, 22, Note: Genesis 3:4.

It is through unbelief that he catches us in his web of destruction. This is verified by the devil's statement: "Hath God said" in Genesis 3:1. Matthew Henry further clarifies such by saying:

> "Thus Satan endeavors to shake that which he cannot overthrow, and invalidates the force of divine threatenings by questioning the certainty of them; and, when once it is supposed possible that there may be falsehood or fallacy in any word of God, a door is then opened to downright infidelity"[2]

In taking a personal survey of many of the born-again churches, I noted that the doctrine of Divine Healing is becoming a lost art among those who were once staunch propagators. Many are sick and seek prayer for healing, yet healing is eluding them. Believers have become shaken in their faith. As I observed the faith in Divine Healing waiver, more and more fall prey to accepting sickness and disease as the will of God. God's solders are acquiescing to the medical evidence given them by medical practitioners. The spiritual battle that needs to be warred becomes too overwhelming on our flesh. In that weak state, we start to think that perhaps I'm not supposed to be healed. Yet, there has been no word from the Lord that our race is about up. When God's soldiers doubt healing as the will of God, we claim sickness as the will of God (Matthew 9:29).

This will be seen in the historical synopsis of Divine Healing in chapter two. The fight of faith is exchanged for subservience to the enemy's lies. Too many Christians are discouraged, disheartened, and have quit fighting. I addressed this in my first book about storms. The reason for the lack of vigor to fight will become more evident as we go on in this book.

It is generally agreed that faith is a prerequisite for all that God's soldiers receive from God, and we will address the application of faith and its importance relating to the concept of this book. While faith plays a major role, this book is to help God's soldiers understand the reason for the demonic activity of sickness and disease that has been unleashed against their physical body.

---

2. Henry, *Matthew Henry's Commentary On the Whole Bible*, Vol. 1, 18–19.

Only as we are enlightened to Satan's strategy will we understand what is taking place. Knowledge equips God's soldiers to counter attack the devil through faith (Psalm 119:42).

In order to have faith to overcome, we have to understand the schemes, the strategies, the plots, the maneuvers, etc. of the devil. It is imperative that we also know the promises of God. If we do not understand that we have the necessary means to defeat and overcome Satan's tactics, we will be overcome by the storms, obstacles, strategies, or ambushes of the devil. We must utilize the arsenal or weapons that we have been endowed with in God's armor or we give place to the devil and his lies. The armor of God is thoroughly addressed in my book, *Faith's Journey Confronts Obstacles: Instructing God's Soldiers to Overcome in His Armor.* I will not deal with the armor here, as this book is meant to build upon my previous books concerning faith.

The Purpose of the Book

The purpose of this book is to enlighten God's soldiers to the satanic stronghold that has developed against the Body of Christ. It is an all-out attack on our health by Satan. As I bring forth in the cyclic pattern of Divine Healing in chapter five, sickness and disease consume much of our thoughts and time. Titus 2:6 tells Christians to be sober minded, however, medication has dulled mental alertness and discernment. Furthermore, prescription drugs have caused reactions worse, in some cases, than what was being treated. Satan has convinced God's soldiers to follow the medical advice given by their doctor and many are worse from side effects than the original disease or sickness. I am not encouraging rebellion against doctors, I am only concerned that we understand God's will for our body. Most of the medical prescriptions are a money-making enterprise for the drug companies and offer no healing for the recipients of the drugs. All the drugs do is cover up the symptoms. They do not encourage the body to be healed. God wants us to understand that He created our bodies to heal itself. When given the correct nutrients, supplements, vitamins, etc.

necessary, our body will react positively and heal itself. This will be explained more as we go on. I am not advocating anything that I have not experienced in my life. If my previous two books have been read, they revealed this truth. God does not want His child sitting as Job and believing that He has forsaken or abandoned us. We place more value and faith in man's wisdom, man's education, man's medicine, etc. than in the God who created our body. He is the one that knows every intricate detail and what is necessary for us to be healthy.

Many medically drugged saints are being strategically lulled into an acceptance of sickness and disease. When God's soldiers become self-conscious, spiritual warfare becomes abated (Matthew 16:24). It is my persuasion that Christians have been given into the hands of Satan (Daniel 7:25; Job 2:6), and the verse in Daniel is the key to the apparent deterioration of the principle (doctrine or teaching) and manifestation of Divine Healing in God's soldiers today.

As Satan waged war against Job's physical body, he is now doing so to the Body of Christ. However, Job had no concept of what was going on. He did not know that God's soldiers have power (authority) over all the power that has been given to the devil (Luke 10:19). Unless, we know what is taking place, we, too, will remain in our smitten condition in an aura of bewilderment. We, as Job, will wonder why God has deserted us (Job 9:1–10:22). When that occurs, we seem to lose any fight that we had and accept the sickness or disease as the will of God. Many times, the devil convinces us that we are at life's conclusion with the severity of the malady. Yet, God gave no such communication that we were to get our affairs in order. God's soldiers must overcome the devil's lies, stand fully equipped in His armor, and trust God for the healing. Prayerfully when this book is read, all will know how to stand and fight for the healing that is God's will.

Daniel 7:25 is a Satanic Plot to "Wear Out" Saints (God's Soldiers)

As Satan was permitted to physically inflict Job, Daniel 7:25 exposes such permission has been granted that will enable him to wear out God's soldiers through bodily affliction. Evidence will be brought forth that clearly delineates a connection between the epidemic of sickness and disease in Christians today and the *wearing out* of the saints prophesied by the prophet Daniel.

I propose that the outbreak of health disorders in the Body of Christ today is a strategic plot of Satan to lull us into accepting our infirmity as the hand of God (Job7:20–21, 9:17). History confirms that the enemy has never worn down the Church of God through persecution. Only when we are continuously attacked with bodily affliction does our faith begin to waiver. It is then that we become weary (worn out). To explain, Job persevered through great adversity. He suffered the loss of his possessions, his servants, and his children, yet Job did not *wear out* until the severe ailment in his body.

My expectation for writing this book is to prove that the generally accepted interpretation of the persecution of Daniel 7:25 is limited in its exegesis. This is not saying that the conventional explanation is incorrect, only that some decisive factors may have been previously overlooked. If God's soldiers understand that Satan is attacking their body and how to take authority over him, bodily healings will once again be part of Christianity.

Chapter two will discuss the important elements that may not have been heretofore contemplated. However, the specifics will become more evident in chapter four, which is the survey of the persecution of the Church throughout history. The true saints of God have never been hindered through great losses or martyrdom. History has revealed prayer and praise by God's soldiers while being beaten, imprisoned, and martyred!

2

Examining Daniel 7:25

Wear out the Saints and Given Into His Hand

An examination does not require a thorough inquiry of a subject. However, it does give license to search for truth. This chapter will concentrate on what may have been overlooked previously in this prophetic verse in Daniel. By inspecting some of the facts and proposing some new insights, the apparent decline in the manifestation of Diving Healing may be illuminated.

Part of the Scripture will be given more consideration. This is not to suggest that any of the verse is less important, but for this book, we are dealing with the increase of satanic attack on the physical bodies of God's soldiers. It is my belief that Daniel 7:25 holds the explanation.

> Through wisdom is an house builded; and by understanding it is established (Proverbs 24:3).

This verse conveys that whatever is being built, whether a house, a family, a belief, etc. it must have a firm foundation in which to catapult its construction.

If a conviction is built as a result of presumption, it cannot be established. Wisdom basis its analysis on truth, and truth is the only wise foundation to build upon. Therefore, it is wisdom that considers the original language used in the Scripture before endeavoring to establish any belief.

A lesson in Hebrew is not necessary when the proper research tools are readily available for God's soldier to take advantage of. According to the Strong's Concordance, the Hebrew word for *wear out* is *BELAW*; means to afflict, wear out, and is used in a mental sense.[1] The word given *(YEH-HAB)* is defined as delivered, give, lay, and hand *(YAD)* is defined as hand, power.[2]

It is my conviction that since Strong's has been a solid resource since 1890, that the definitions are solid in their interpretation. However, for the sake of those who might question, I did search other word studies. Each time, I found that the original language was basically defined as those given in Strong's Concordance.

The affliction implied in Daniel 7:25 is to be in a mental sense. It is, therefore, safe to conclude that Satan will mentally afflict (wear out) the saints of God. Defining the word affliction reveals that it is the state of being afflicted, a state of pain, distress, or grief. Causing continued or durable pain of body or mind, grieving, distressing.[3]

Through this meaning is communicated that the *wear out* under consideration will be a lingering and long-wearing pain, grief, or distress. This was adequately demonstrated in the book of Job. According to this information, it is safe to propose that the general analysis of the wearing out of the saints in Daniel 7:25 may be further interpreted. This will be discussed later in this chapter in more detail to explain and illuminate what Satan is currently doing to God's soldiers. However, for now, it is necessary to move on to the next item of research.

General Theological Consensus of Daniel 7:25

Research reveals insufficient comment by diverse theologians concerning any in depth evaluation of *wear out the saints* and *given*

1. Strong, *The New Strong's Exhaustive Concordance of the Bible*, 21, Hebrew Dictionary Number 1080.

2. Ibid., P. 47, 3052, 3028.

3. Webster, *American Dictionary of the English Language*.

into his hand. However, it was deemed necessary to quote some of the comments to show the brevity of what has been previously considered. The emphasis by most commentators was placed on the time element of Daniel 7:25. Although I will consider their thoughts, the important factor will center on defining what up to now may not have been considered.

A very reliable commentator through the years has been Matthew Henry who states:

> "He shall wear out the saints of the Most High; he will not cut them off at once, but wear them out by long oppressions and a constant course of hardships put upon ruining their estates and weakening their families . . . And in these daring attempts he shall for a time prosper and have success; they shall be given into his hand."[4]

Another like Matthew Henry that would be considered an old faithful is Albert Barnes who said:

> "This would be a persecuting power: 'and shall wear out the saints of the Most High,' ver. 25. That is, it would be characterized by a persecution of the real saints–of those who were truly the friends of God, and who served him . . . It would continue for a definite period: 'and they shall be given into his hands until a time and times and the dividing of time,' ver. 25. They; that is, either those laws, or the people, the powers referred to. Maurer refers this to the 'saints of the Most High,' as meaning that they would be delivered into his hands."[5]

I have not given the statements that these great men gave in their discussion of the time frame in Daniel which is their belief that it refers to the three and a half years of the tribulation. However, I will quote the exposition in the Pulpit Commentary. The expository dissertation by J. E. H. Thompson enlarges the generalized thought of time and times and the dividing of time; he goes beyond the orthodox stipulation of the three and a half years of

---

4. Henry, *Matthew Henry's Commentary on the Whole Bible*, 844, Vol. 4.

5. Barnes, *Barnes Notes*, 72–73.

the tribulation period held by most of the commentators. Here is Thompson's exegesis of the verse:

> "Shall wear out the saints of the Most High. Persecute them, or maintain war against them; the natural meaning of the word is "afflict." . . . And they shall be given into his hand until a time and times and dividing of time. Who shall be given into his hands? It is usually assumed that it is the saints; but the LXX asserts that it is universal dominion that is given into the hands of the oppressors. We have no right to assume that *IDDAN* "a time" means "a year;" IT IS ANY DEFINED TIME. Certainly it does approximate to the time during which the temple was polluted with heathen offerings; but it also coincides with equal accuracy to the campaigns of Vespasian and Titus against the Jews. Vespasian landed in Galilee in the beginning of A.D. 67, and Jerusalem fell on September 5, A.D. 70. There was thus, approximately, three years and a half occupied by this war. But "centuries" might last be meant. From the birth of our Lord, on whom the oppression was first exercised, till the accession of Constantine, was three centuries and a portion of a century."[6]

What seems to materialize in the commentaries cited is a presumed thought that the affliction of the saints will be a continual or constant persecution by Satan relating to the Tribulation Period. Statements by other theologians were almost as brief and related the general thought of those mentioned. Although this author's belief does not seem to be one previously considered; some of their remarks do give license to discuss another interpretation.

Additional Theological Interpretation of Daniel 7:25

Scripture, many times, has a twofold implication. It is called the *law of double reference.*

---

6. Thompson, *The Pulpit Commentary*, vol. 13, 219.

While it is conclusive that a reference points to a specific event, it gives allusion to another. With this thought in mind, let us continue to lay the foundational evidence for the evaluation that God's soldiers need to consider.

It is probable according to the criteria mentioned in the exposition of the Pulpit Commentary that time in Daniel 7:25 could be referring to more than the common acceptance of three and a half years. Since *IDDAN* (time) is an appointed time, it can refer to something other than the tribulation. What is preventing us from saying that this would involve a specific period (e.g. Christ was born at the fullness of time, the appointed time that God's foreordained knowledge chose for His birth, Galatians 4:4)?

A certain time frame was allocated before Christ would be born. There seems to be a similar metaphor in the time of the saints wearing out. It will cease at the fullness of time which is the end of the period allowed for this particular persecution. Each of the examples stated is an appointed time according to God's timetable.

It is my staunch belief that only as God's soldiers are willing to keep God out of a box where previous dogmas have been kept, that the Holy Spirit may advance us to new heights of Biblical illumination and interpretation.

> For laying aside the commandment of God, ye hold the tradition of men, as the washing of pots and cups: and many other such like things ye do (Mark 7:8).

Donald C. Stamps has this to say concerning this verse in Luke:

> "The Pharisees and the teachers of the law were guilty of placing human tradition above God's direct revelation. They followed their own laws and regulations even when those things were not consistent with the standards of God's word . . . Traditions or rules must be based on, and remain consistent with truths found in the Bible.[7]

Many may have eyes to see, but do not perceive because we allow the leaven of the Pharisees to overrule the direct revelations of God's word. God's soldiers accept the legalistic restraints of those

7. Stamps, *The Fire Bible, King James Version*, 1480, note 7:8.

teaching them and never search the Scriptures to see if it is sound doctrine. To be reliable, a doctrine must be backed up by various Scriptures. Several take a Scripture out of context and base doctrine on it. In their complacency to accept as true what is taught, those listening are impeded in their spiritual growth. God wants us to search the Scriptures and make sure that something taught balances with the whole of His word and not taken out of context.

I will endeavor to reveal what I believe about time through a knowledge of Scripture and historical happenings. Hence if time is any time deemed to accomplish a particular phase or level, then time can be defined as that period which is needed to fulfill a desired stage. This makes no rules of restriction that limit the time to a certain amount of days, weeks, months, years, etc. It only states that a time is that which involves certain qualifications before entering another time.

This author is not disputing that the three and a half years of time is not an implication to Antichrist and the tribulation period. What I am suggesting is that the time could have a double reference that has not been hither to speculated. With this, a possible explanation involving what the time, times, and dividing of times might be referring to in this double reference will be advocated.

In as much as this book primarily focuses on resolving the reason for the deterioration of the manifestation of Divine Healing in the Body of Christ, the first period (time) will begin with the Fall of Man (which was not only the beginning of Satan's reign as the prince of this world, but the initiation of sickness and disease into the human race) and end with Abraham. The second period (time) will be from Abraham to David. The third period (time) will be from David to Christ. The half period (time) will be between Christ's ascension and the new heavens and earth. This will be Christ's second coming to set up the Messianic Kingdom before the millennium (which will be the conclusion of Satan's reign as prince of this world and the end of sin, sickness, and disease).

A calculation of the time involved in each period will reveal an inconsistent number of years; however, the periods are not based on a strict rule of years. The periods (times) are the fullness of the time needed for God to complete that facet of His plan before going on to His next phase. In other words, period (time) is simply the fullness of time (time frame, period) that God allocated for each particular purpose, phase, or plan to take place. God has given everything a season, and a time to every purpose under heaven (Ecclesiastes 3:1–8).

Daniel 7:25 makes clear that God's soldiers will be given into the hands of the one wearing them out. That means that God has given Satan power to afflict His people for the allowed period (time frame). Satan has been oppressing God's people through persecution, adversity, losses, grief, etc. since the beginning of there being a people of God.

I want to reiterate that I am not soliciting a dispute of any rapture of the church teachings or any tribulation period beliefs. This author is only concerned with awakening the insight for the deterioration of the manifestation of Divine Healing in God's soldiers. God has not changed and neither has His word.

The stimulus anticipated from this book is that consideration be given to the possibility that Satan will not only do his ultimate "wearing out of the saints" during the tribulation period, but it could be referring to more than that. I believe that Daniel 7:25 could also address the satanic oppression of sickness and disease against believers today, which is the prerequisite for the ultimate assailment on the saints of God during the generally accepted interpretation referring to the tribulation period.

> But let him ask in faith, nothing wavering. For he that wavereth is like a wave of the sea driven with wind and tossed. For let not that man think that he shall receive any thing of the Lord (James 1:6–7).

It is the affirmed belief of this author that Satan, who has the power to inflict sickness and disease, has many in the Body of Christ afflicted. As Job, they sit in confusion and bewilderment, while growing too weary to engage in spiritual warfare. Once steadfast in their faith concerning Divine Healing, now their continued malady, the negative teaching on healing, medical science, and confusion has caused their faith to be tossed about like a blade of grass in the wind. As is stated in James, the result is that healing is not received. In chapter six, I will give insight into how healing can be hindered because of man's medical knowledge. Faith must supplant man's knowledge, man's wisdom, man's education, etc. if healing is to take place.

> And Satan answered the Lord, and said, skin for skin, yea, all that a man hath will he give for his life. But put forth thine hand now, and touch his bone and his flesh, and he will curse thee to thy face. And the Lord said unto Satan, Behold, he is in thine hand; but save his life (Job 2:4–6).

In the book of Job, it is evidenced that Satan was given permission by God to inflict bodily disease (skin for skin). In other words, Job was given into the hands of Satan. Likewise, Daniel 7:25 reveals that the saints of God are given into the hands of Satan. It is quite clear that he has been given power to wear them out. As previously shown, the wearing out will be through severe mental affliction. In the survey of church persecution in chapter four, history will show that no matter how severe the persecution has been, the saints have never worn down through it. A study of Scripture affirms that same fact.

With the criterion brought forward, I believe that an additional theological evaluation of Daniel 7:25 is in order. It is evident that Satan will use his usual strategies of calamity, adversity, war, persecution, grief, losses, etc. to try to wear out God's soldiers. However, as revealed, his most strategic plot to wear down the saints is through infirmity in their physical body. It is further believed, by this author, that Daniel 7:25 is not an isolated incident involving the three and a half years of the tribulation period.

I am convinced that it has a double reference to the power that Satan has now. At the present time, he is diabolically inflicting the saints of God with an onslaught of sickness and disease. This will continue to be an easy vendetta for demonic powers, unless God's soldiers awaken to the lies about Divine Healing and the accepted preconception of Paul's thorn being any hindering disease. This will be further discussed in chapter three.

Yes, death, as of yet, has not been destroyed (1 Corinthians 15:26). Howbeit, God has given the saints power (authority) over all sickness and disease (Luke 10:19). I believe that this is backed up by Daniel 7:26 which says that God passed down a ruling that gives the saints authority to take away Satan's dominion. Consequently, the only enemy that has God's permission to overrule the authority that God's soldiers have is their time of death. Paul, Peter, etc. had authority over all the power of the devil (Satan) until it was time to let death have its way!

3

An Observation of Divine Healing

With all that has been written about Divine Healing, much of the information will not be necessary for this book. It is not needed to give a thorough dissertation here. For this work, the discussion of Divine Healing will concentrate on the data which the author has appraised applicable to the contemplated belief. In other words, the discussion will be focused around those facts which the author has judged necessary to indicate that another implication is found in Daniel 7:25.

Satan: The Source of Sickness and Disease

Distinctly connected with Satan's personal agency are found sickness and disease. The story of Job gives a clear view of the source from which he obtained his malady. Satan was the direct instrument of Job's bodily torment (Job 1:6–2:7). It is the theme upon which Jesus based His teachings. In the Gospels, Jesus definitely attributed the sickness and disease of His time to direct satanic power. It was Satan who had bound the woman for eighteen years in Luke 13. Man has been under satanic attack on his physical body throughout history.

At this time, it is wise to ascertain where man's physical assault first began. It is found in Genesis chapter three, where Satan is exposed as being the instigator of man's Fall. Here, man's spiritual and physical being were affected when he became corrupted by sin. Before the Fall, man did not die physically, and he was spiritually alive. There was no need to be regenerated or born again. This truth is expressed in 1 Peter 2:24 where the apostle quotes the prophet Isaiah. Peter's intention in quoting Isaiah 53:5 (which literally means healing has happened to us) was to reveal that personal wholeness: mental, psychological, physical, and spiritual flows from man's conversion. The word "healed" used by Peter means to heal or to be made whole. To explain, the Atonement of Christ takes into consideration the twofold nature of man, the Fall's effect on the double nature, and man's need for both spiritual and physical salvation or deliverance. Peter was signifying that physical healing as well as spiritual healing took place on Calvary.

It is evident that the cause of disease and suffering can be distinctly traced to the Fall and man's sinful state. There was no sin, sickness, or disease before man fell in the garden. Since disease is part of the curse of sin and the result of man's Fall, it must be embraced in the provisions of redemption. This truth will become clear as we go along.

God: The Source of Divine Healing

It is in the cross of Jesus Christ that redemption finds its center. The fundamental principle of Divine Healing rests on the atoning sacrifice of Christ. If sickness is the result of the Fall, then it has to be included in the Atonement of Christ, where on the tree, He "Himself took our infirmities and bare out sicknesses" (Matthew 8:17). A. J. Gordon, an outstanding Baptist minister of the nineteenth century and the founder of Gordon College in Boston, saw the Atonement as a foundation for faith in healing:

"In the Atonement of Christ there seems to be a foundation laid for faith in bodily healing, seems . . . we say, for the passage of Matthew 8:17 is so profound and unsearchable in its meaning that one would be very careful not to speak dogmatically in regard to it. But it is at least a deep and suggestive truth that we have Christ set before us as the sickness bearer as well as the sin bearer of His people . . . In other words, the passage seems to teach that Christ endured vicariously our diseases as well as our iniquities."[1]

Scripture proclaims loud and clear that God is the source of Divine Healing, and that He promises to heal His children. This affirms health even if God's soldiers do not want to include healing in the Atonement. However, to reject healing as part of the Atonement, means the Christian is denying the efficacious work of Calvary which the Scriptures claim included the whole man (Isaiah 53:3–5; Matthew 8:17; 1 Peter 2:24). The Bible expresses that God's ultimate will for His soldiers is that we "be in health, even as thy soul prospereth" (3 John 2). According to Jesus, sickness is contracted by satanic means. It is cured by the supernatural intervention of God with or without the use of earthly means. God will either heal immediately through anointing with oil and laying on of hands, or He will direct to organic means that will enable the body to heal itself. This will be addressed more as we go on. At present, we are concerned with the verity that Satan is inflicting the infirmity and that Jesus is the Healer. A. B. Simpson puts it plain enough:

"It was demonic influence that held and crushed the bodies and souls of those Christ delivered. If sickness is the result of a spirit agency, it is most evident that it must be met and counteracted by a higher spiritual force and not by mere natural treatment."[2]

God proclaimed, "I AM THE LORD THAT HEALETH THEE" (Jehovah-Rapha, Exodus 15:26). This is affirmed in Psalm 103:3) by the Psalmist who states:

1. Bailey, *Divine Healing: The Children's Bread*, 45.
2. Simpson, *The Gospel of Healing*, 27.

"Who forgiveth ALL thine iniquities; who healeth ALL thy diseases."

It is quite clear from this Psalm that the scope of healing promised is to include all that needs to be healed. The text confirms physical healing, since the Hebrew word *TACHAWLOO* (diseases) is from the same root *CHAWLAW* as the word for (disease) in Exodus 15:26 where *MAKHALEH* revealed God to be the Healer of diseases. Furthermore, the words for heal which is *RAPHA* are the same in both passages where the distinct meaning involves the idea of mending or curing.[3] These two verses give ratification that God is the Healer of the whole man. He forgives ALL sins, and He heals ALL diseases.

Because God is the Source of healing, He gives His solemn promise to keep sickness and disease away from His soldiers, as cited in Psalm 91:9–10:

> "Because thou hast made the Lord, which is my refuge, even the most High, thy habitation; there shall no evil befall thee, neither shall any plague come nigh thy dwelling."

In that Scripture is found an incredible promise of protection from sickness and disease as a blessing of the redeemed life. The word for plague *NEHGAH* is used for something "inflicted" specifically on the physical body. Howbeit, the protection is conditioned upon God being the true refuge and habitation. That means that God's soldiers make God a place of trust and flee to Him for protection. As God becomes our ONLY security (refuge), we are protected from sickness and disease.[4]

Although the Divine Healing promises have been quoted mainly from the Old Testament, the New Testament makes no bounds to declare that God is the same yesterday, today, and forever (Hebrews 13:8). His promises are a sure foundation. Heaven and earth may pass away, but His word will stand forever (Matthew 24:35). These verses expound that the God who promised

---

3. Hayford, *Spirit Filled Life Bible*, 841.

4. Ibid., *Spirit Filled Life Bible*, 833.

healing in the Old Testament has not changed His ability, nor has His word changed in its stability. God's word is sure and certain. God, who cannot change, will not alter His word. What He promised yesterday, stands today, and forever.

Faith: The Basis for Receiving Divine Healing

Whether the disease is spiritual or physical, the cross of Christ has set the believer free (John 8:36). God's soldiers must grasp hold of the fact that by Christ's cross, the dominion of sin (and all its power, strength, authority, domination, faculty, etc.) has been broken and we are no longer slaves to sin, sickness, disease, poverty, etc. Why does there seem to be little trouble in believing there is freedom from sin's power in the Atonement, and so much controversy and trouble in believing there is also freedom from the power of sickness and disease in the Atonement? The answer is quite simple when considering the truths dispersed through Scripture. It seems that most have a little concept of God; unbelief was why Jesus did not many miracles in Nazareth (Mark 5:5–6).

As lack of faith hindered the working of miracles in Jesus' hometown (Matthew 13:54–58), so unbelief in God's soldiers still hinders the working of His power (Matthew 9:29). Ephesians 2:8 trumpets that salvation is experienced through faith. Here, it must be understood that salvation carries with it the connotation of deliverance. This means to be set free or to be liberated from any form (all types) of bondage. Notwithstanding, Ephesians also clarifies that the deliverance or liberation will only be achieved through faith.

The question that arises is how do God's soldiers achieve the faith that necessitates the salvation or deliverance? As the word of God gave us the prerequisite for obtaining salvation, it does likewise for obtaining the faith required for deliverance. According to Romans 10:17, faith is obtained through hearing the word of God. Faith must always rest on the Divine word. The most important element in the "prayer of faith" is a full and firm persuasion that the healing of disease by simple faith in God and His ability to perform what He promises is a part of the gospel and a doctrine of the Scriptures.

When God delivered Israel from Egyptian bondage (that which had them captive), He promised to keep all the diseases of Egypt from them as long as they would keep His commandments. Sickness belongs to the Egyptians, not to the people of God. God's soldiers must grasp hold of this reality. We seem to be aware of the future benefit of bodily resurrection, yet too few understand the present redemptive benefit the body can realize in this life.

The problem is that our old nature (the flesh) and our new nature (spirit) are contrary to each other (Galatians 5:17). That's why when we are forgiven, we still question our forgiveness at times. Just as God's word makes clear that whatever sin we confess is forgiven (1 John 1:9), it makes clear that healing also belongs to God's soldiers (Jeremiah 17:14; Deuteronomy 7:15; Acts 10:38; Psalm 103:2–3). Unbelief is conquered by the truth of the word of God. The more of God's word that we ingest, the stronger our faith can become. Jesus made clear that they were healed physically by their faith (Luke 7:50; Mark 10:52; Luke 17:19). The devil wants us to believe that the infirmity has been sent to us by God which will cause us to doubt healing and accept the sickness, disease, illness, etc.

God is not the author of sin and sickness. These are the diabolical instruments designed by Satan to destroy (John 10:10). God has designed forgiveness and healing as the merciful blessings to redeem man and make him whole. The restoration of health (Psalm 41:3), the making whole or well whether physically, mentally, or spiritually is God's will for His soldiers (3 John 2). If He is our God, He is our Healer of the whole man. He cannot divide Himself (separate His nature). To be Jehovah-Rapha means God is our Healer, or else He is not our God. In my second book, *Faith's Journey Confronts Obstacles: Instructing God's Soldiers to Overcome in His Armor*, I clarified the foundation of faith and that if we believe God, He can do anything.

An Historical Synopsis of Divine Healing

The first narratives of Divine Healing are found in the Old Testament. In the Genesis period are several recordings of God physically healing the problem of infertility (Sarah, Rebekah, and Rachel). A little later in Exodus 15:26, God makes His covenant of Divine Healing with Israel. This took place at Marah where God had sweetened the bitter water. The sweetening of the bitter water is associated with the ordinance of healing that God gave. The healing tree used was a symbol of the Lord Himself. This let God's soldiers know that if we abide in the redemptive covenant, we are assured of protection from disease, as well as healing. This covenant is not pledged to Israel only, but to all of God's children whether Old Testament, New Testament, or today.

In Leviticus, the laws of health clearly illustrate that God's healing us is not to be considered as an unconditional blessing. As we must walk in fellowship and obedience to God, we are to conform to the precepts that regulate healthful habits and diets which are of His creational design. Proper diet, adequate sleep, exercise, and cleanliness are as much a part of the Bible doctrine of Divine Healing as is anointing and prayer. God's soldiers have an obligation to give proper care to their bodies.[5] The necessity of obedience is again brought out in Deuteronomy. Here Moses reiterated that as obedience brought blessings, the consequences of disobedience would bring the opposite. These results incorporated the diseases of Egypt.

The Psalms of David contain a theology of healing. In them is shown that healing the body of disease is a benefit of redemption. Contained in the blessing of healing is found recovery from disease, deliverance from the grave, and renewal of physical vigor. David makes a strong statement in Psalm 103:1–5 where he declared that he was redeemed from the ultimate outcome of his sickness, which suggests that David accredited Divine Healing to the atonement. His son, Solomon, communicates in his Proverbs that he had an in-depth understanding of the doctrine of Divine

5. Bailey, *Divine Healing: The Children's Bread*, 132.

Healing (Proverbs 3:7–8). This probably came through his father's Psalms.

Taking a look at the books of the Kings, Elijah (through invoking God's hand) raises the son of the widow of Zarephath (1 Kings 17:17–24). Elisha prays and the woman from Shunam is healed of her barrenness (2 Kings 4:14–17). Later on, Naaman, the captain of the army of Syria, was cleansed (healed) of leprosy by Elisha (2 Kings 5:1–14). Further, when Hezekiah was smitten with a fatal illness, he was healed in answer to his own intense prayer to God (2 Kings 20:1–6).

Of all the Old Testament references on Divine Healing, one of the most astounding incidents is found Daniel 4:36. In this narrative, Nebuchadnezzar was healed of mental illness. After living in such an incredibly unproductive condition for seven years, the Lord so healed him that he was completely restored to a normal life. Undoubtedly, this indicates that God heals the mind as well as the body.

In the New Testament is found the Healer of the Old Testament incarnate and walking the earth. Christ is found healing an impotent man at the pool of Bethesda (John 5:1–16), healing the centurion's servant of palsy (Matthew 8:5–13), healing Peter's mother-in-law of a fever (Matthew 8:14–15), healing those who were blind, lame, lepers, deaf (Matthew 11:5), raising Jairus's daughter from the dead (Mark 5:22–43), and the list goes on.

After Jesus' physical ministry, we find the early Church being a healing Church. Jesus was healing, but through His Church. Although it was God's soldiers physically laying on hands, speaking the word, etc., it was Jesus working through the Holy Spirit in them to do the healing. The first miracle of physical healing mentioned was by the Apostle Peter. This was the healing of the lame man at the gate beautiful (Acts 3:1–8). Plus, Peter is seen healing Aeneas who was paralyzed for eight years (Acts 9:32–33). Later, we find Paul being healed from the bite of a poisonous viper on the Island of Melita (Acts 28:1–6). After the pagans had seen this miracle, Paul laid hands on the father of the ruler and he was healed (Acts 28:7–9).

It would be wise to note that the ministering of healing was not restricted to the Apostles only. References of laymen such as Stephen, Philip, and Ananias recount that they were used by the Lord to heal physical disease. Ananias was sent by God to heal Paul of his blindness incurred on the Damascus road (Acts 9:10–18). Jesus promised that such signs would follow ALL who believed in His Name (Mark 16:17). The early Church took this seriously and they received results. Faith in action produced an extraordinary number of healings that gave no doubt that Jesus meant healing to be an ongoing practice in His Church.

The Ante-Nicene Church did not see the doctrine of healing as just some dogma handed down from the Apostles. The Church fathers connected the phenomena of physical healing with the doctrine of the resurrection. In light of the resurrection of the body, it was obvious that Christ through His Name should heal sick bodies. They believed the physical body was redeemed and could expect to experience the privilege of redemption in some degree before the ultimate glorification of the body.

The writings of the first three centuries verify the practice of the ministry of healing continued after the Apostles. One of these writers was Origen who wrote:

> "We assert that the whole habitable world contains evidence of the works of Jesus, in the existence of those churches of God which have been founded through Him by those who have been converted from the practice of innumerable sins. And the name of Jesus can still remove distractions from the minds of men, and expel demons, and also take away diseases."[6]

Justin Martyr referred to Isaiah 53:5 "through whose stripes ye are healed" by stating that the manifestation of power in actual incidents of healing was attributed to Christ's death and resurrection. In his Apology II to the Senate, he commended Christ to them because of the profound and prevalent cases of healing and

---

6. Bailey, *Divine Healing: The Children's Bread*, 202.

deliverance. Although the cases were considered incurable, healing was effected in the Name of Jesus.[7]

Between 412 and 428, Cyril of Alexandria in his book "Worshipping in Spirit and Truth" referred to anointing and prayer for healing. He urged Christians to avoid sorcery and magic in the recovery of illness. They were to renounce such practices, look to God, and call for anointing as recorded in the book of James.[8] In A. D. 709 and 716, Bede in his commentary on the book of James, testified to the use of anointing in the Church of England in his own time and the remarkable healings that had occurred as a result of this practice by writing:

> "And let them pray over him, anointing him . . . We read in the Gospel that the apostles also did this; and at the present time it remains the custom of the church, that the sick should be anointed by the presbyters with consecrated oil, and that anointing being accompanied by prayer, they should be restored to health."[9]

These early soldiers of God knew that "oil" typified the work of the Holy Spirit, who is the Agent in healing. That is why their "prayer of faith" was effective. When they anointed, they expected God to keep His covenant of healing. They believed God's word that says:

> But without faith it is impossible to please him: for he that cometh to God must believe that he is, and that he is a rewarder of them that diligently seek him (Hebrews 11:6).

About the ninth century, the ordinance of anointing for physical healing changed from an ordinance for physical healing to a sacrament designed to prepare believers for death.[10] In fact, until the Church's restoration movements which began about 1500, the Church birthed and established by Jesus lost most of its original and experiential truths. Its supernatural demonstrations had

---

7. Ibid., *Divine Healing: The Children's Bread*, 202.

8. Bailey, *Divine Healing: The Children's Bread*, 204.

9. Ibid., *Divine Healing: The Children's Bread*, 206.

10. Ibid., *Divine Healing: The Children's Bread*, 206.

deteriorated from a brilliant thousand-watt searchlight to a flickering one-watt candle.[11]

The Church had lapsed into a religious monument practically devoid of the truths of Scripture, not only in belief, but in practice. Except for the spurious claims of healing, magic and witchcraft abounded. Therefore, it opened the door for the plagues of Egypt. Epidemics of smallpox, cholera, bubonic plague, etc. overtook man. Sickness and disease literally had its way. Thousands upon thousands died with each successive outbreak. Satan was malevolent in his strategy to destroy through sickness and disease.

It is evidenced that the authority over satanic powers given to God's soldiers was forfeited through disobedience and unbelief. Christ, who had redeemed us from the curse of the Law (Galatians 3:13), was grieved at the spiritual poverty ruling those who were supposed to be believers. God had forewarned His soldiers of such sickness and disease in Deuteronomy 28, where He listed the blessings and curses. Among the curses that would come through disobedience (unbelief) would be consumption (tuberculosis), fever, inflammation, extreme burning, emerods (tumors), scab (any disease of the skin), itch, madness, blindness, ailment of the knees and legs, great plagues of long persistence, sore sickness of long persistence, all the diseases of Egypt, also every sickness and every plague which is not written in the book of the Law. Thus, without the light of Scripture, the Church, as Job, sat bewildered by her infliction of physical disease for about a thousand years. She had forgotten Jehovah-Rapha (the Lord her Healer).

It wasn't until the time of the Reformation that the Church of England abandoned the Roman doctrine of extreme unction and returned to the practice of anointing for physical healing, which the Reformers believed to be apostolic. One of these, Martin Luther, the great German Reformer, personally had a strong faith in Divine Healing. He not only encouraged prayer for the sick, but also practiced it in his own life. Both his wife, Katherine, and his coworker, Melanchthon, were saved from death by God's healing touch in answer to prayer.[12]

---

11. Hamon, *The Eternal Church*, 106.

12. Bailey, *Divine Healing: The Children's Bread*, 214.

At the beginning of the eighteenth century, the Anabaptists made an impact upon the religious life of Europe and Germany, in particular.[13] Many of them revived the practice of anointing the sick with oil. Also the Mennonites, who were part of the Anabaptist movement, practiced anointing as a result of an inductive study of the Scriptures.

The doctrine of Divine Healing was not officially restored to the church until about 1800. This was during the peak of the Holiness Movement. The Methodist Church of America was one of the first to be touched by the healing movement. Some outstanding Methodist theologians and Church administrators became exponents of Christ, the Healer.[14] The founder of Methodism, John Wesley, was quoted by Rev. Charles J. Fowler about his statement concerning the permanence of healing in the Church:

> "This single conspicuous gift (of healing) which Christ committed to his Apostles remained in the Church long after the other miraculous gifts were withdrawn. Indeed it seems to be designed to remain always, and St. James directs the elders who were the most, if not the only gifted men, to administer it. This was the whole process of the psyche in the Christian Church till it was lost through unbelief."[15]

Moreover, in his diary, Wesley recorded several incidents of Divine Healing. Among which was found an interesting entry written in 1784. Wesley noted that after leaving Taunton, one of the horses became lame. Knowing that he could not obtain any human help, he prayed for the horse and the lameness went away. Not only confirming Jehovah-Rapha as Healer of His people, but substantiating the fact that the healing covenant included the livestock of God's soldiers (Deuteronomy 28:4).

By the turn of the nineteenth century, interest in the truth about healing was at a high in evangelical circles. In America, the teaching of Divine Healing attained wide acceptance. The

13. Ibid., *Divine Healing: The Children's Bread*, 214

14. Ibid., *Divine Healing: The Children's Bread*, 221–222.

15. Bailey, *Divine Healing: The Children's Bread*, 221.

movement knew no denominational bounds. The doctrine was embraced by the Episcopalians, the Baptists, the Congregationalists, etc. In almost every segment of the evangelical community, the practice of anointing for healing was endorsed.

Each decline in the practice of Divine Healing is remarkably satanic in origin. However, this particular low is really incredible. According to Keith M. Bailey, the churches advocating healing cowered about the 1930's. He stated that the excesses practiced among some Pentecostals brought many of the churches to silence on this doctrine. They were afraid that the teaching on healing would identify them as Pentecostal.[16] This is mind boggling that they chose to stay sick and diseased because of a fear of being tagged as Pentecostal. Instead of anointing and praying, they accepted sickness as the will of God. The devil will stop at nothing to get God's soldiers to doubt the Scriptures. Fear of being considered to go along with the Pentecostals, caused those staunch believing denominations of Divine Healing to cower to the devil and receive his sickness and disease. That indicates that they chose to accept whatever the devil inflicted their bodies with because of an aversion to the Pentecostals.

Outside of a few highs, a decline or negative sentiment in the practice of Divine Healing seems to have continued to the present. Apparently, the opponents outnumber the proponents of the doctrine. Objections such as: the age of miracles is past, the miracles of Christ and His apostles were designed to establish the facts and doctrines of Christianity and are not needed today, if these things are so, people should never die, Paul was not healed, and so on. Whatever the objection may be, negativism has bred absurd unbelief. Many now pray, "If it be thy will to heal." As soon as God's soldiers question if it is God's will to heal, they have encouraged unbelief. Yes, there is a time to die, but only God knows whose time is up. Unless God has made clear that He's calling us home, pray with faith for healing. This is distressing that the Church has come so far away from the Apostolic Church belief that God is Healer. My prayer for this book is that it will again cause the

16. Ibid., *Divine Healing: The Children's Bread*, 228.

Church to awaken to the truth that Divine Healing belongs to all of God's soldiers.

Paul's Thorn and Sick Trophimus
Headline Healing Negativity

Ludicrous as it seems, the opponents of Divine Healing use Scripture to encourage unbelief. If ever there was an artifact used to plague doubting Christians, it is Paul's thorn in the flesh as recorded in 2 Corinthians chapter twelve. Then to add fuel to the fire of unbelief, these false teachers erect as some great monument, the story of Trophimus left sick in Miletum (2 Timothy 4:20). As these obstacles stand before them, Christians plunge readily into Doubting Castle, the place where Bunyan's Christian and Hopeful found themselves through unbelief. Once inside, doubt allowed Giant Despair to almost thrash them to death.

Before deliberating about Paul's thorn, consideration will be given first to Trophimus being left in Miletum sick. This verse is heralded by the opponents of Divine Healing as a front page advertisement. It's sort of like today's Fake News so prevalent that downplays any truth. At first glance, it appears that the famous Apostle Paul had to leave his friend behind because of illness. As expressed earlier, death is the only enemy left to be put under. Such could be the case here. If it was Trophimus' time to depart, death would have its way. Nonetheless, to help the skeptics to read on, let's assume, in light of Scripture, such to be questionable. This is drawn from 2 timothy 4:6 where Paul wrote that he knew his time for departure was at hand. It appears reasonable to assume that he would have stated something of the sort for Trophimus.

The fact that Paul, in such a casual manner, gives his statement in 2 Timothy 4:20 after mentioning that Erastus stayed at Corinth, communicates that he did not consider it unusual. Yet, the ONLY mention in the New Testament of anyone remaining behind because of sickness is rather unique. At this, I believe that consideration should be given to the word "sick" in that verse. According to Strong's Exhaustive Concordance and Vine's Expository

Dictionary, the word "sick" implied to be feeble (in any sense); literally to be weak, impotent, diseased, sick; to have negative strength.[17] It must be noted that this can be weakness without disease.

Searching the Scriptures gives no inclination as to the age of Trophimus. Since the Greek word for sick is not restricted to disease, but has a broader significance, 2 Timothy 4:20 could have been translated as: "but Trophimus have I left in Miletum weak." This reveals that he may have been unable by nature to execute the task of making the trip. With that in mind and his age unknown, it would be safe exegesis to say that Trophimus, because of old age, was unable to make the journey with Paul. The point that I am stressing is to throw out the doctrine of Divine Healing over the mention of one not making the journey with Paul is rather preposterous.

Now, consideration will be given to Paul's thorn in the flesh (2 Corinthians 12:7). Evidence reveals that Scripture is quite allusive when it comes to a conclusion as to what Paul's thorn may have been. Nowhere is his thorn defined. All that is definitive is that it was the *messenger of Satan* to buffet him. To explain, there was a demonic force that contended against Paul. It was something that continually opposed him. It is certain, however, even if the thorn was a kind of physical infirmity, it brought the power of Christ to rest upon Paul mightily. To this, Matthew Henry states:

> "This thorn in the flesh is said to be a messenger of Satan, which he did not send with a good design, but on the contrary, with ill intentions to discourage the apostle (who had been so highly favored of God) and hinder him in his work. But God designed this for good, and overruled it for good, and made this messenger of Satan to be so far from being a hindrance that it was a help to the apostle."[18]

---

17. Strong, *The New Strong's Exhaustive Concordance of the Bible*, 16, Greek Dictionary #770. Vine, *Vine's Complete Expository Dictionary of Old and NT Words*, 573.

18. Henry, *Matthew Henry's Commentary on the Whole Bible*, 517.

The onslaught of sickness and disease in the Church has not been the result of heavenly visions and profound revelations. To use Paul's thorn as an excuse for accepting sickness as an obstruction to do God's will is pride. Perhaps, self-exaltation prompts such mentality. Paul's thorn was the direct result of his heavenly vision and visit to the third heaven, where he heard things unlawful for a person to utter (2 Corinthians 12:1–7). The messenger of Satan was permitted to keep him humble.

A look at Scripture explicitly gives no inclinations that Paul's thorn in the flesh kept him bedridden, kept him in the hospital, kept him from accomplishing any of his journeys, kept him away from any meetings, kept him from prayer and study of the word, kept him so medicated that he could not think straight nor function properly, or kept him from writing or dictating his renowned epistles. As a matter of fact, it is clear that Paul was not limited or hindered in any way from fulfilling his apostolic call. To be clear, his thorn in the flesh was not debilitating. God did not incapacitate Paul to keep him humble. He performed whatever had to be done and effactually accomplished his ministry for the Lord. How many Christians today have a severe physical malady or thorn in the flesh and are still an incredible witness to the power of God in their life? One that comes to my mind is Joni Eareckson Tada. She demonstrates the grace of God being made perfect in weakness as her life exhibits the power of God to perform the call God has given her.

Let's understand that if we are hindered in accomplishing our ministry to the Lord, we have been deceived by the enemy. I am not saying that we may not be overcome by a sickness or infirmity. What I am saying is that if it stops or completely prohibits us from doing our mission for Christ, we are accepting what is not of God. If God's soldiers are prohibited from doing what He has called us to do, it is NOT a thorn in the flesh. Paul was not hindered from accomplishing his ministry for the Lord. Paul's thorn was to keep him humble, but it did not disable him. Whether our ministry is prayer, teaching, preaching, helps, etc., any continuous impediment in the performance in our duty to Christ, because of an infirmity, is proof that we are not being humbled by God. To say otherwise, would be to indulge in the exaltation of self, which gives no glory to God.

Whenever there is a continuous inability to achieve our duty to God, we are deceived. I am not saying that we may not be afflicted with a physical malady, but it will not be a permanent situation that keeps us from doing what God has called us to do. Even in a wheel chair, God's soldier can accomplish God's call. To think that we must be incapacitated by a so-called thorn is a satanic misconception of humility. Acceptance of any "thorn" that hinders God's soldiers from doing our Godly mission must be repented of. This is nothing more than pride and unbelief. God gives grace to the humble and rejects the proud (James 4:6). No foothold should be given to the devil (Ephesians 4:27). God's soldiers must believe that God is Jehovah-Rapha and that He rewards those who expect to receive from Him (Hebrews 11:6).

It is obvious that sometimes God may give us a thorn in the flesh to keep us humble, but His grace will enable us to go on in spite of the thorn. It will not interfere with His work. Paul was not hindered from performing his ministry. He made clear that the grace of God was sufficient for him to do the will of the Lord. If we magnify our thorn or infirmity and use it as an excuse to be remiss in our walk with Christ, it means that we are living below the grace of God.

I am aware that this is perhaps difficult to understand, but please stay with me to the end of the book. As we go on, things will become more clear. In the meantime, let me give an example of anointing and praying for healing. When my youngest daughter, Christina was about twelve, she was running a fever. I didn't know that she was not well until I had come home from work. When I saw her, I asked her what was wrong. She just said that she felt weak. I took her temperature and it was 102°. I immediately told my husband that we have to get her to the hospital. Suddenly, she began to convulse, her eyes were rolling back into her head, and she was turning blue. The hospital was too far away, so I cried out to the Lord in a panic. The Lord very plainly impressed me to trust

Him, to anoint her, and to pray. I grabbed the oil, anointed her, and prayed. She seemed to get worse, and I cried out, "Lord, I believe, please help my unbelief. My God, if you don't touch her, she is dying." I then felt a strength in my spirit and cried out, "In the Name of Jesus, devil get your hands off my baby. She belongs to Jesus and you have no part with her." Immediately, she stopped convulsing, her eyes became normal, and the fever was gone. God wanted me to step out in faith. How could I preach to others about healing, unless I truly believed that He is Healer?

God wants His soldiers to understand that He has never changed, He is the same yesterday, today, and forever (Hebrews 13:8). Jehovah-Rapha healed in the Old Testament, the New Testament, and He is still Healer today. If it is not our time to be called home, we must believe in the God that heals. In other words, we must believe in the God that heals unless He has made clear that we are going home.

Healing is the children's bread and we are to be whole. Why some are given a thorn in the flesh that appears that they are not healed is not made clear in the Bible. It only claims that it is to keep humble. However, no matter the severity of the thorn, it is indicative that the recipients exhibit the power of God in a mighty way in their life. That is definitely proven in Paul's life and in Joni's life. In short, a true thorn in the flesh will demonstrate the power of God in a potent way in that life.

Let's continue with Paul. We see that through his thorn in the flesh, he learned the magnitude of God's grace. Not once was he unable to accomplish his duty to God. In fact, the Scriptures are ambiguous in their clarification of the exploits achieved by Paul. In spite of his thorn in the flesh, he was enabled to rise as more than a conqueror through stripes, prison, stoning, shipwreck, perils, hunger, cold, and so on (2 Corinthians 11). It is certain that anyone picturing Paul as a feeble invalid unable to perform his apostolic duties is spiritually blind in one eye and cannot see out of the other. As a matter of fact, the Bible says:

> And God wrought special miracles by the hands of
> Paul: so that from his body were brought unto the sick

handkerchiefs or aprons, and the diseases departed from them, and the evil spirits went out of them (Acts 19:11–12).

Consequently, this illuminates further the false interpretations God's soldiers may use in excusing themselves from being healed. If we actually had a similarity to Paul's thorn in the flesh, we should be acknowledged for how mightily the Holy Spirit uses us. Unless this claim can be made, it is time for us to see that some demonic activity has us deceived. Jesus, in Luke 10:19, gave God's soldiers authority or power over ALL the power of the devil!

4

A Survey of
Church Persecution

To FULLY COVER THE subject of the persecution of the Church, it would probably take the writing of a multi-volume work. Although the subject of this book is not developed around Church persecution, it is necessary to give adequate information about persecution to convey that it does not hinder Christianity's growth. It is the concern of this author to establish a belief in regard to Daniel 7:25 and the deterioration in the manifestation of God as Healer in the Church.

This chapter will embrace sufficient evidence of the persecution of God's soldiers throughout history to give claim to the proposed view. It is my staunch belief that the persecution previously pondered involving Daniel 7:25 has overlooked the important factor that persecution has never weakened God's soldiers. Unless, a connection is given between the verse in Daniel and the widespread epidemic of sickness and disease in the Church, many will continue to be prey to satanic destruction of the physical body. A revelation of the persecution in Daniel 7:25 will reveal that it is not only meant for the tribulation period. It is my conviction that Satan is working his diabolical plot and inflicting "wearing out" God's soldiers with sickness and disease today. He has been ambushing us with physical illnesses since the Fall of man in the Garden of Eden. As long as we sit as Job and believe that our physical ailment is from God or that it is God's will, the devil will keep us from recognizing that it is him that is inflicting us and not God. I am convinced that by the time this book is read, all God's soldiers will be more armed to put the devil to flight.

If you have not read my other two books, it would be helpful to understand how the devil works and how to overcome him. *Storms Are Faith's Workout: Preparing Christians for Spiritual Ambush* will lay the foundation of God's love, how the devil works, and how to overcome him. Once the book is finished, God's soldiers will come away with an understanding of God's love, with the knowledge to overcome the storms, and how to be standing when the storm has ceased. *Faith's Journey Confronts Obstacles: Instructing God's Soldiers to Overcome in His Armor* will reveal how faith works and the necessity for the full armor of God. When the book is read, God's soldiers will have learned how to use God's armor, will be emboldened to confront any obstacle, and will overcome it by faith in His armor.

Why the Church is Persecuted

Before getting into this next topic, I would like to make a suggestion to God's soldiers who wish to gain an overview of Church persecution. Such an overview may be achieved by viewing "The Trial and Testimony of the Early church," a video curriculum by Gateway Films.[1]

In spite of severe persecution, history reveals that Christianity not only met persistent and often sever persecution in its first centuries rising to a crescendo early in the fourth century, but that it spread and was even strengthened by the persecution. The tradition of martyrdom has entered deep into the Christian

---

1. Gateway Films, *The Trial and Testimony of the Early Church: From Christ to Constantine*, Approximately 3 hours.

consciousness. With the possible exception of Judaism, Christianity has had more martyrs than has any other religion.[2]

Jesus Christ, the Head of the Church, made distinct declarations in the gospels concerning persecution, such as:

> Think not that I am come to send peace on earth: I came not to send peace, but a sword (Matthew 10:34).

> Remember the word that I said unto you, The servant is not greater than his lord. If they have persecuted me, they will also persecute you; if they have kept my saying, they will keep yours also (John 15:20).

> Ye shall be hated of all men for my name's sake (Mark 13:13).

Words like that give reason to believe that God's soldiers (those who believe and follow Christ) will be persecuted. Jesus made known that while His followers are in this world, they will be hated, persecuted, maligned, and rejected for His sake.

The early Church was not left comfortless when opposition arose and continued against her, God's soldiers had the words of Christ and His pledge that He would never leave nor forsake them (Matthew 28:20). On His promise that they would overcome all obstacles by faith, the Church was sustained (1 John 5:4). Only through Christ could these infant believers survive. As Jesus had warned, persecution was their lot. Numerous arrests, court trials, attempts at browbeating, threats, flogging, martyrdom, and jailing were continuously before them.

An absolute antagonism existed between Christians and the world. There was conflict between the spiritual empire of Christianity and the fallen empire of Judaism, as well as the heathen empire of Rome.[3] Both the Jewish and Roman religions were at the opposite ends of the spectrum with respect to Christianity. No settlement was possible. God's soldiers based their faith on Jesus, the true God and Messiah. The Jews had rejected Him who was

---

2. Latourette, *A History of Christianity*, Vol. 1, P. 81.

3. Sheldon, *History of the Christian Church*, Vol. 1, PP. 133–134.

their only means of salvation. Rome based her religion on false gods of all origins.

Because they were fundamentally different from all other religions, God's soldiers suffered at the hands of the world. Believers in Christ are not of this world. Our citizenship is in Heaven (Philippians 3:20). We have different values, standards, and priorities. The direction of our life is in opposition to the world's system. Those of us in Christ refuse to compromise with the ungodly standards of this world. We have set our affections on those things which are above, and not on things on the earth (Colossians 3:2).

God's soldiers know that friendship with the world means to be at enmity with God (James 4:4). If we are for God, we must be against that which is contrary to Him and His word. Scripture is adamant that there is only one way to God, and that is through Jesus Christ (John 14:6). The early Church adhered to this Biblical stance which denounced all other religions. Since they refused to recognize any other religion, they were considered to be trouble makers and anti-socialists. Because the heathen world saw God's soldiers as a threat to civilization, they favored the extinction of Christians.

Christianity had given a mighty blow to satanic dominion, and it had to be stopped any way deemed suitable to the apostate mind. For the first time in history, God's soldiers had the upper hand. Satan had failed in silencing their leader. Christ rose triumphantly, spoiling principalities and powers, and made a show of them openly (Colossians 2:15). The prince of this world had lost ground that he secured from Adam after the Fall.

Now, the enemy of the cross of Christ was desperate in his hatred for God and His soldiers. Satan craves to be god, but God's soldiers refuse to let him be such in our lives. Motivated by hatred, he stirs up animosity in his followers to attack Christianity. As a matter of fact, the prophet Isaiah quoted Lucifer's desire to place his throne above that of God's. With his desire to be god, God's beautiful cherubim had placed himself superior to his Creator (Isaiah 14:13–14). The Apostle Paul in 2 Thessalonians 2, also, recites the devil's obsession to be god. Desiring to be worshipped by the whole of God's creation, Satan will sit in the temple of God and claim to be god. His desire for the worship of mankind is an obsession that has blinded him of any conception of truth.

The only obstacle hindering mankind from worshipping him as god is the believers in Christ who will put no other god before God (Exodus 20:3). Is it any wonder that he would rally all the forces of hell to bring down the Church? However, Christ has promised that the gates of hell will not prevail against it (Matthew 16:18). Satan deceived himself, when as a cherub, he became a hearer only of God's word (James 1:22). Once self-deceived, he actually thought he could stop Jesus. Although he didn't stop Him, his self-deluded thinking thought he could stop the Church from doing the will of God. Hence, in his derangement, he incited the Jews and the heathen Rome to stamp out the early Church at any cost.

As God's soldiers read about the early Christian Church, we find that Christianity survived while the odds were all stacked against it. Such mounting disadvantages should have kept the Church's increase at a minimum. Yet, the spread of Christianity in its earliest centuries is one of the most amazing phenomena in all of human history. Beginning in Jerusalem, it was mainly comprised of ordinary working men and women with no spectacular abilities. Spreading to Rome, the majority of the Roman Christians, even down to the close of the second century, belonged to the lower ranks of society. Despite their lowly positions, the Early Church was enabled by Christ to accomplish extraordinary tasks of self-denial and walk the martyr's road.

Although Rome was a mighty persecutor of Christianity, it is not Roman authority that first instigated persecution against the infant Church. The New Testament discloses the fratricidal conflict in existence between Jews and Christians, the latter challenging the Jews by claiming to be "the New Israel."[4]

4. Frend, *Persecution in the Early Church, Christian History*, 6.

Jewish Persecution of the Church

On the message of an expectation of persecution, Jesus commissioned His Church (Matthew 10:16; John 15:20). For long centuries, that was to be God's soldiers experience in the world. The persecution began by the skeptical sect of the Sadducees, who took offense at the doctrine of the resurrection of Christ, the center of all apostolic teaching.[5]

Soon Ecclesiastical authorities realized that Christianity offered a threat to their prerogatives as interpreters and priests of the law. At this, they united their forces to combat the "new religion." Rome had given the Sanhedrin, a politico-ecclesiastical body, permission to supervise the civil and religious life of the state.[6] They were not about to allow these "Christians" to interfere with their Roman authority.

Intent on silencing the "sect," the Sanhedrin had Peter and John hailed into their presence. Upon standing before this august group, the apostles were warned and forbidden to continue in their preaching of the gospel (Acts 4:17–18). The Jewish leaders would not tolerate anything that contradicted their teachings. To accept the teachings of the Christians would be an admittance that they had their "Messiah" murdered by the Romans. The thought of such an acknowledgement was inconceivable to the Jewish leaders.

During this early persecution, Christianity was provided with its first martyr. Stephen, who had been chosen with the seven to administer the charitable funds of the Jerusalem Church, was brought before the Sanhedrin. False witnesses, unable to gainsay the spirit and logic with which he spoke, accused him of blaspheming Moses. After a remarkable address in his own defense, in which he denounced the Jewish leaders for their rejection of Christ, he was stoned by the mob (Acts 6–7). Thus, Christianity had its commendable leader of the venerated army of martyrs.

The stoning of Stephen gave the first taste of Christian blood. With this, the enemy now thirsted for more, and a general

---

5. Schaff, *History of the Christian Church*, Volume 1, P. 249.

6. Cairns, *Christianity Through the Centuries*, 56.

persecution of the Church followed. The cause and the Kingdom of Christ were at stake. The faithful followers of Christ were as a small flock of helpless sheep set upon by a pack of hungry wolves. The broken Church at Jerusalem was in a dreadful predicament and the prospect of God's soldiers seemed to be dark and gloomy. However, with its members scattered in every direction, it gave way for the spreading of the Christian faith throughout Palestine and the surrounding region.

After about seven years of repose, the Jerusalem Church suffered a new persecution under King Herod. His motives stemmed chiefly from a political stance. Wanting to keep peace with the Jews, Herod had James, the brother of John, beheaded. Seeing how this act pleased the Jewish leaders, he then imprisoned and condemned Peter to the same fate. However, Peter was miraculously liberated by God who had other plans for him (Acts 12:1–17).

Jewish persecution of the Church resulted primarily from the belief that "only" the Jews serve the True and Living God. Where Judaism failed was in the rejection of Jesus Christ as the Messiah. Christianity claimed to worship the Messiah of the Jews. This infuriated the Jews, who considered themselves the interpreters of the Scriptures. They were not looking for a crucified Savior. Theirs was to be a mighty king sitting on the throne of David. Unless, a Jew becomes born again, this conflict remains between the Jews and the disciples of Christ, even today.

Roman Persecution of the Church

This section will be quite lengthy. In order to maintain sufficient evidence to confirm this author's belief that persecution breeds believers, I will elaborate upon Roman persecution. History reports no mightier, longer, and deadlier conflict than the extermination waged by heathen Rome against Christianity.[7] Roman persecution was severe enough to prove that Daniel 7:25 is referring to more than the persecution generally attributed to that verse.

---

7. Schaff, *History of the Christian Church*, 33.

According to History, it is revealed that the Roman religion was not intolerant of different religions. Into its pantheon, Rome had accepted deities from the Italian tribes and from Asia Minor. In the provinces, the great territorial gods, such as Saturn of North Africa and Jehovah among the Jews, were accepted as being legal religions on the grounds that their rites, even if uncivilized, were hallowed by ancient tradition. Worshipped by the ordinary inhabitants of the Greco-Roman world, were countless local gods and goddesses. These were often provided with a classical equivalent name and worshipped as "Roman" deities.[8]

At first the Church was considered to be part of Judaism, which was sanctioned as a legal sect. When Christianity was distinguished from Judaism as a separate sect that might be classed as a secret society, it came under the ban of the Roman state. Despite their forbearance of other religions, the Roman state would brook no rival for the allegiance of its subjects. Now recognized as an illegal religion, Christianity was considered a threat to the safety of the Roman Empire.[9]

Christianity was a religion which aspired to universality. The Kingdom of Christ was to be set up throughout the whole earth. Romans regarded the state as the chief thing. They would promote religion only in as far as it served the interests of the state. The state was the highest good in a union of the state and religion. Because the Christians held no sympathy with this idea, their enemies lost no opportunity to represent Christianity as dangerous to the state, which brought upon them the enmity of the Roman rulers.[10]

On the moral and spiritual loyalty of those who accepted Christ, the Christian religion was exclusive in its claims. When a choice had to be made between loyalty to Christ and loyalty to Caesar, Caesar had to take second place. According to the leaders of Rome, who were rigid in preserving classical culture within the framework of the Roman imperial state, Christians were seditious. Rome saw much of the Christian practices as blatant infidelity to

8. Frend, *Persecution in the Early Church*, 5–6.

9. Cairns, *Christianity Through the Centuries*, 87.

10. Newman, *A Manuel of Church History*, 149.

the state. Christians consistently refused to offer incense on the altars devoted to the genius of the Roman emperor, with whom the welfare of the state was inextricably mingled in the minds of the people.

Christ's followers withdrew themselves from social intercourse with the pagans; this was rendered necessary because of the idolatrous practices connected with every aspect of life. They refused to participate in idolatrous rites and to frequent the temples. The influential classes hated the Christian religion. Believers were thought to be atheists and enemies of the gods. As enemies of mankind and of the gods, believers were regarded with the profoundest abhorrence by the people in general.[11]

In addition to their "strange" behavior, God's soldiers had no idols and little visible paraphernalia of worship. Believers excluded from their homes and their persons all symbols of idolatry. The Roman state religion was mechanical and external which included altars, idols, priests, processionals, rites, and practices that people could see. Because Christian worship is spiritual and eternal, believers stood and prayed with their eyes closed. With no visible object to which those prayers were addressed, the Romans considered them as unbelievers. Romans were accustomed to symbolic, material displays of their gods.

Negativity, being the prevalent consensus of the Romans, opened the door for devious allegations against the Christians. Because of the popular hatred, nothing was too bad to be credited to the believers. Holding their meetings at night in secret gave way to further suspicion and false accusations. The Roman authority conceived this secrecy as meaning the hatching of sedition against the safety of the state. Assembling at night and being observed for their fondness of each other brought moral charges against them. Rumors spread making them guilty of incest, cannibalism, and unnatural practices.

The unbelievers misunderstood the meaning of "eating and drinking" the elements that represented Christ's body and blood. Christians were accused of killing and eating infants in sacrifice

11. Newman, *A Manuel of Church History*, 149.

to their God. The charge of incest and other types of immoral conduct, repugnant to the cultured Roman mind, resulted from the Christian "kiss of peace" offered in brotherly love. Of course, not one of the charges were justified. A study of Scripture would have revealed such behavior to be anti-Christian, and condemned by God. The enemy, however, was not going to refute any of the practices that could have hindered his spread of ungodliness.

Christianity came into conflict with the temporal interests of certain classes, such as priests, vendors of sacrificial animals, makers and vendors of idols. Many persecutions were provoked by such persons who saw the Christian faith as an impediment to their success. In whatever way the Church could be persecuted, her enemies formed the attack. The occurrence of famines, earthquakes, military reverses, fires, etc., frequently furnished occasion for the persecution of the Christians, who, as enemies of the gods, were supposed to be the cause of the evils.[12]

Because Christianity was recruited primarily from the poor and the outcast, it was looked down upon by those who would be regarded as respectable. To the proud Roman aristocracy of wealth, power, and knowledge, the gospel was despised as a vulgar superstition.[13] This is not surprising when considering the Scriptures which claim:

> For ye see your calling, brethren, how that not many wise men after the flesh, not many mighty, not many noble, are called: But God hath chosen the foolish things of the world to confound the wise; and God hath chosen the weak things of the world to confound the things which are mighty; And base things of the world, and things which are despised, hath God chosen, yea, and things which are not, to bring to nought things that are: That no flesh should glory in his presence (1 Corinthians 1:26–29).

It is, therefore, no monumental revelation to see that the upper class of stiff-necked and uncircumcised Romans would consider the Church as an illegal and depraved religion.

12. Newman, *A Manuel of Church History*, 150.
13. Schaff, *History of the Early Church*, Volume 1, 373–374.

The Christians were known to despise the Roman gods. They were loyal subjects of a higher King than Caesar. Satanic powers rose up through the hierarchy, and Rome rushed into deadly conflict with the Christian religion, and opened, in the name of idolatry and patriotism, a series of repeated persecutions. Storm after storm of suffering was unleashed by this tyrannical government to annihilate the Christian Church.

The demonic influence infiltrating Rome rose high in the Emperor Nero who became the most prominent persecutor of the new religion. Yet, the early years of Nero's reign were not unfavorable to the spread of the gospel. Son of the ambitious and intriguing Agrippina and stepson of the simpleton Emperor Claudius, he succeeded to the imperial dignity while still a youth. Gifted in poetry and in music, good-natured, humane, the beginning of his reign awakened high expectations. The youthful Nero, sometime after his assumption of the purple, rejoiced that not one drop of blood had been shed in his entire empire.[14]

The transformation of the brilliant, trusting Nero into the cruel monster started about A. D. 55, when he ordered the murder of his brother Britannicus. In A. D. 60, his mother, at his command, was assassinated. The divorce and ensuing murder of his first wife Octavia and the death of Poppaea, his second wife, from personal abuse, represent stages in his downward career. The world was to him a comedy and a tragedy, in which he was to be the chief actor.[15] Being insanely greedy of praise for his poetic and musical accomplishment, he played the part of a court jester to gain the popular applause. His sanity was dethroned by unbridled indulgence in vice of every description, the flattery of corrupt favorites, and the possession of unlimited power.

Nero was the first who attacked, with the imperial sword, the Christian sect. His tyranny prepared the flaming portal through which the Christians entered upon a long and painful ordeal of incredible persecution. Eusebius Pamphilus describes the atrocities of this Roman emperor thusly:

14. Newman, *A Manual of Church History*, 112, Volume 1.
15. Schaff, *History of the Christian Church*, 378, Volume 1.

> "To describe, indeed, the greatness of this man's wicked-
> ness . . . as there are many that have given his history in
> the most accurate narratives, everyone may, at his plea-
> sure, in these contemplate the grossness of his extraordi-
> nary madness . . . And, indeed, in addition to all his other
> crimes . . . he was the first of the emperors that displayed
> himself an enemy of piety towards Deity . . . Thus, Nero
> publicly announcing himself as the chief enemy of God,
> was led on in his fury to slaughter the Apostles."[16]

The martyrdom of the Apostles Peter and Paul in Rome about A.
D. 64, the tenth year of Nero's reign occurred during his first imperial persecution. Paul was beheaded and Peter was crucified upside
down. Crucifixion upside down was requested by Peter. He did not
feel he was worthy to die in the same manner as his Lord.

The fearful inferno of Rome, the most destructive and disastrous occurrence of history, was one of Nero's hellish spectacles.
Sometime in the month of July in the year 64, Nero had Rome
set on fire. For six days and nights the fire burned. The greater
part of the city laid in ashes.[17] Of the fourteen regions into which
the city of Rome was divided, only four remained unscathed.
Temples, monumental buildings of the royal, republican, and imperial times, the richest creations of Greek art which had been collected for centuries were turned into dust. Men and animals were
incinerated by the flames. The metropolis of the world became a
cemetery. To divert attention from himself as the diabolical plotter
of the devastating fire, he malevolently cast the blame upon the
Christians. This man was like a demon in human form destroying
for his amusement.

When their Emperor claimed the Christians had done the
devastation, the people arose with cruel hatred to have the "so
called" guilty Christians punished. Thus, there began a festival of
blood such the like of which heathen Rome had never seen before
or since. This was the retaliation of the powers of hell to the Holy

---

16. Pamphilus, *The Ecclesiastical History*, 80.

17. Kuiper, *The Church in History*, 61.

Ghost preaching of Peter and Paul who had shaken heathenism to its core.

So insidious was Nero, that he played the role of the faithful Emperor who was relieving Rome of the pernicious Christians. Once accused with the crime of setting the fire that destroyed ten regions of the Roman city, Christians were arraigned. A vast multitude was convicted, not so much on the charge of arson, as for their hatred of the human race. Their deaths were made more cruel by the mockery that accompanied them. An innumerable multitude of Christians were put to death in the most shocking manner. Women were tied to mad bulls and dragged to death. Some were sewed up in the skins of wild beasts and exposed to the voracity of mad dogs in the arenas; many perished on the cross or in the flames.[18] There was no end of the ways that were used to kill God's soldiers.

The epitome of this satanic endeavor took place at night in the Emperor Nero's imperial gardens. Christian men and women covered with pitch, oil, or resin, and nailed to posts of pine, were lighted and burned as torches for the amusement of the mob; while Nero entertained them in capricious apparel and play acted his art as a charioteer. Only a madman could have been guilty of the follies and atrocities committed by this Roman emperor.[19]

The second and the third centuries found many of the emperors to be men of great moderation. One should expect that such would put an end to Christian persecution. However, these men adhering more rigidly to the laws against unauthorized religions, in some instances, incurred the most violent persecution. Because of the anxiousness to maintain the splendor of the old religion, they were more repelled by the fanatical proceedings of the Christians.

During the reign of Marcus Aurelius (161–180), Christians suffered more severely under him than any emperor since Nero. To him, their enthusiasm was mere fanaticism. He did not look at their steadfastness under persecution as fidelity to a high principle; he saw it as obstinacy in disobedience to the constituted authority

18. Kuiper, *The Church in History*, 61.

19. Newman, *A Manuel of Church History*, 113, Volume 1.

of Rome.[20] This emperor decreed that the property of Christians should be given to their accusers. Everywhere there were people who were eager to have the property of the Christians. These came forward with false accusations. Christians were sought out, brought to trial, and often executed with the greatest cruelty, while their property was taken from them and given to their accusers.[21]

The happenings to the Church in Lyons and Vienna in southern Gaul, now France, give some idea of the severity of the persecution under Marcus Aurelius. The persecutors began by insulting the Christians; they threw stones at them and plundered their homes. And finally, by the most horrible tortures, they sought to make the Christians deny their faith. All day long they tormented them, until the tormentors had to give up because of utter exhaustion.[22] Hatred for Christians during his reign was further inflamed by the extraordinary catastrophes that took place. Earthquakes followed by famine and pestilence, insurrections and invasions on the frontiers involving the empire in almost continuous and often disastrous war, aroused the fury of the masses against the Christians whose irreverence and rapid increase was thought to have angered the gods.

These persecutions were a determined and systematic attempt to uproot Christianity completely, and wipe the Church off the face of the earth.[23] Everywhere, Christians were put to a test of their faith. The execution of Christian leaders and the demolition of the Christian houses of worship were the means most frequently taken. However, the ability of Christianity to withstand the most determined assaults of the greatest world power known to antiquity, was fully displayed and gave to the Church the complete confidence of supreme victory.

---

20. Ibid., *A Manuel of Church History*, 156, Volume 1.

21. Kuiper, *The Church in History*, 63.

22. Ibid., *The Church in History*, 63.

23. Ibid., *The Church in History*, 66.

The Toleration of Christianity

Satan consumed with the destruction of God's soldiers changed his tactics in the fourth century. Up to this time, he raised up emperors determined to discard the believers of Christ. In turn, the rulers instigated the populace to hatred of the Christians. The progression of persecution led to the multiplication of believers. Persecution tended to spread rather than suppress Christianity. Satan had to deviate to other means of destruction. His attack was to use the sanctioning of Christianity to bring about its downfall.

The Roman army in Britain proclaimed Constantine emperor in 306, giving him rule over Britain, France (then Gaul), and Spain. Italy and North Africa were ruled by Maxentius who wanted to be emperor over the whole of the western part of the Roman Empire. War broke out between the two, but Constantine's army was three times smaller than that of Maxentius. Included in Maxentius's army were the flower of all the Roman armies, the Praetorian Guards.[24]

Constantine was in a dangerous situation. Believing he needed supernatural help, he invoked the help of his god (Mithra the Persian sun-god). The evening before the battle, he saw a cross above the sun with letters of light saying, "In this sign, conquer."[25] He claimed that night to have a dream or vision that confirmed that he was dealing with the God of the Christians. On October 28, 312, the day after the supernatural phenomenon, his army won a momentous victory over the army of Maxentius.

Constantine did not formally adopt Christianity as a religion of the state, he merely gave it an accepted position due to his political interest. Through Christianity, he gained popularity with those he depended on for the support of his government. He was a shrewd and unscrupulous politician who can hardly be supposed to have exercised a saving faith. A Christian man would not have

---

24. Kuiper, *The Church in History*, 68.

25. Ibid., *The Church in History*, 69.

murdered nearly all his relatives, including his nephew Licinianus, his son Crispus, and his wife, Fausta.[26]

The three sons of Constantine are declared to be more positive in furthering the Christian faith than their father. They had been instructed in this faith, and favored its spread. Such prolonged patronage by the Emperors enabled the Christian communities to grow rapidly. However, many were motivated by other than religious conviction to be admitted into the Church. Joining the Church could mean official favor and even wealth. The wickedness of man was now being clothed in religious garments (Matthew 7:15). In other words, the Church was full of whited sepulchers full of dead men's bones and all uncleanness (Matthew 23:27). There was nothing righteous in the motives of those joining the Church, thereby corrupting any evidence of the Church that was founded on the doctrines of the Apostles of Christ.

By the time of the middle ages, Christianity is secularized. Her Churches assumed the majesty of the heathen temples. So wide were the doors of the Church open, that any distinction between the world and Christianity had been erased. Most of the influential Christians had been brought up as pagans. Christianity was adopted because it was the vogue thing to do.[27]

With the influx of pagans into Christianity came their paganistic practices. Unless man is changed on the inside, his outer actions will remain the same (John 3:3). Pagans worship their gods in the form of images. To accommodate the "new converts," the churches were filled with statues and images. Of course, these paganistic gods must have Christian names. Select names as, Mary, the mother of Christ, the apostles, and noted martyrs took on the form of idols. These idols became recipients of the prayers of the people. Forgotten were the words of Jesus who said that whatsoever you ask in my name, that will I do, that the Father may be glorified in the Son (John 14:13).

It is revealed through history that with great power and influence, the Christian Church of Rome became a persecuting power,

---

26. Newman, *A Manuel of Church History*, 308, Volume 1.

27. Ibid., *A Manuel of Church History*, vol. 1, 308.

making use of the civil authority for the suppression of anything that interfered with her authority. Salvation was now accomplished only through the Church. Yet, the Bible makes clear that salvation is in Christ alone, for there is none other name under heaven given among men, whereby we must be saved (Acts 4:12).

The Old Testament was looked upon as being the model of Church polity. Represented as very pleasing to God was the persecuting zeal of the Old Testament rulers. Now, those who slaughtered multitudes of heathen. Destroying their places and objects of worship, were given special adoration. The deterioration or decline of the Spiritual Church is described quite adequately by Dr. Bill Hamon:

> "The Church had changed its nature, had entered its great apostasy, had become a political organization in the spirit and pattern of Imperial Rome, and had taken its nose dive into the millennium of dead works, formalism, and slavery to man-made religion. In other words, it had gone into slavery to a religious Pharaoh and "Egypt" system as Israel had gone in her Egyptian bondage, treading the slime pit of self-works and building great edifices to house a dead religion with none of the life and reality of the Early Church."[28]

Satan, obsessed with power, was the influence that ruled the Church. No longer was she considered as "Holiness unto the Lord." This heathen form of Christianity was void of any resemblance to the Church initiated by Christ. Years of corruption had raised the Church of Rome into the largest pagan religion in the world. Only flickers of truth remained here and there. But God who is rich in mercy would keep His Church (Matthew 16:18). Satan had not won, for on the brink of the horizon, Christ was about to revive His Church. Buried in the ruins of idolatry, traditions of men, paganistic worship, etc., God was awakening those seeking truth to rise up from the shambles.

28. Hamon, *The Eternal Church*, 90.

Unveiling the Hierarchy Church Finds Christian Persecution

God has always had a remnant who will not bow down and worship Baal (1 Kings 19:18; Romans 1:4–5). Found within this Roman artifice were those whose hearts were after God. Many were discontented with Papal authority and false doctrine. A discussion of all the contributors would be too lengthy for this book. However, this author wanted to give honor to those who will be unnamed, and mention that there were many who helped unveil the tyranny of the Roman Church.

Aware that his maneuver to self-destruct the Church was being uncovered, Satan moved, once again, through those who were his, to silence the rebels. In the name of the Roman Church true believers were named as heretics. Many were violently murdered by this demonic hierarchy. Hoping he could frighten them into recanting, Satan held back no punches to annihilate the Church built upon the truth of Jesus Christ.

It was discontentment within the Church that laid the groundwork for the Reformation. The true Church was being raised up in the "so called" Church, which was nothing more than the Roman Empire in the likeness of a magnificent Church. As early Rome, this new Rome was ruthless in its dealings with those who spoke out against its authority. As I previously stated many can be credited with discontent in the Roman Papacy. However, only a few of the martyrs and the cruelty they suffered will be mentioned. Persecution is a concern in this book, only as it influences the belief that Daniel 7:25 is referring to something more than what has been considered in the past.

The first martyr is John Hus who was influenced by the writings of John Wycliffe. It seems that Bohemian students studying in England took Wycliffe's ideas back to Bohemia where they became the foundation for the teaching of John Hus. Desiring to reform the Church in Bohemia, he proclaimed the beliefs of Wycliffe. Earning papal enmity, Hus was ordered to go to the Council of

Constance. Declaring that he appealed not to the Pope but to Christ, Hus stated:

> "Verily I do affirm here before you all, that there is no more just or effectual appeal, than that appeal which is made unto Christ, forasmuch as the law doth determine that to appeal, is no other thing than in a cause of grief or wrong done by an inferior judge, to implore and require aid and remedy at a higher judge, to implore and remedy at a higher judge's hand. who is then a higher judge than Christ?"[29]

The council condemned both his and Wycliffe's views. Hus would not recant. By order of the council, he was burned at the stake on July 6, 1415.[30] According to Gateway Films video (John Hus), he is recorded as singing, "Jesus, thou Son of David, have mercy on me" as the flames consumed him.[31]

It was during the Zwinglian movement that the Anabaptists appeared. Basing their concepts on the Bible, Anabaptists refuted infant baptism. They believed that only believers are biblically baptized. Zwingli who had earlier stood in this belief, gave it up when the insistence on believer's baptism endangered his plans for enlisting the slow-moving conservative authorities on the side of the reform. Zwingli wanted to compromise on the grounds of unity. Nowhere does Scripture allude to compromising its truth for the sake of unity. In fact, the Bible is clear that there can be no fellowship between Christ and Belial (2 Corinthians 6:15). The Anabaptists believed that concession was unacceptable to the integrity of Christianity and were more concerned with the veracity of God's word. Because of the Anabaptists staunch stand for truth, Zwingli followers rose up to persecute them.

Because the eyes of this dark world cannot bear the clear light of the word of God, Anabaptists were cruelly victimized by both Protestants and Catholics. They were burned, hanged, beheaded, and drowned. Howbeit, great men of faith headed this noble

---

29. Foxe, *Foxe's Book of Martyrs*. 113–114.

30. Latourette, *A History of Christianity*, 669, Volume 1.

31. Gateway Films, *John Hus*, 55 minutes.

group. Balthasar Hubmaeir, adopting the ideas of the Swiss radicals, was banished to Moravia where he assumed leadership of the thousands of converts to Anabaptist views. In 1528, the emperor ordered him burned at the stake. His wife was then drowned in the Danube by Roman Catholic authorities.

Michael Sattler, the renowned South German Anabaptist gave a notable witness of the faith at his trial. Reading his discourse in Hans Hillerbrand's "The Reformation," pictures him like Stephen before the Sanhedrin. As Stephen, he answered with such wisdom that his accusers seemed like fools. Angered by his boldness, the judges sentenced him to be executed. Before he was burned to ashes as a heretic, his tongue was cut out, followed by further inhumane treatment to satisfy their demonic personalities. His fellow brethren were executed, and the sisters drowned. A few days following Michael's death, his wife was drowned.[32] This author believes that viewing "The Radicals" by Gateway Films[33] will enlighten the belief that is proposed concerning Daniel 7:25. The film brings forth that persecution will not stop Christians from serving Christ. If torture does not "wear out" the saints, then there could possibly be something else that the Scripture in Daniel is revealing.

Because Anabaptists insisted on the separation of Church and state, the authority of the Bible, and believer baptism, they were considered to be radicals. Yet, despite horrendous persecution, the Anabaptist movement spread from Switzerland to Moravia, Holland, and other lands. It was their free-church concept that influenced Puritan Separatists, Baptists, and Quakers. Anabaptists are the spiritual ancestors of today's Mennonite, Amish, and Hutterite Churches.[34] Such growth, once again, proves that persecution breeds believers.

William Tyndale, a reformer from England, translated Erasmus's Greek Testament into English. Being hindered from the publication of such, he moved to the continent. His English New

---

32. Hillerbrand, *The Reformation*, 238–241.

33. Gateway Films, *The Radicals*, 99 minutes.

34. Cairns, *A History of the Christian Church*, 308.

Testament was published in 1525 in the city of Worms. Although he faced insidious resistance and embittered persecution, seven editions of the New Testament and part of the Old Testament was published in English. When his enemies caught up to him, he suffered a martyr's death on October 6, 1536. As he was being prepared at the stake, he prayed with a loud voice, "Lord, open the King of England's eyes."[35] His prayer was answered in 1611, when the King James Bible was sent forth among the people of England![36]

35. Foxe, *Foxe's Book of Martyrs*, 135–152.

36. Gateway Films, *God's Outlaw–The Story of William Tyndale*, 93 minutes.

5

REEXAMINATION REVEALS THAT DIVINE HEALING HAS A CYCLIC PATTERN OF HIGHS AND LOWS

Persecution Has Never Weakened, But Strengthened the Church

IT SEEMS AS THOUGH the doctrine of Divine Healing has been like a roller coaster throughout Church history. As seen in chapter three, it obviously has had a cyclic pattern of highs and lows. During the lows there is a pronounced lack of healings in God's soldiers. It is obviously due to a lack of conviction in God's word. In that same chapter, John Wesley was quoted as saying the whole psych of the Church was that Divine Healing was designed to remain always. However, it was lost through unbelief. Wesley's conclusion is one of importance when considering the belief determined by the author for this book. With Wesley's analysis and the information brought forward in chapter three, Church history vindicates the position that the withdrawal of physical healing in the Church would suggest a low spiritual condition (a lack of faith in Divine

Healing) among believers.[1] As Satan deceived Eve (Genesis 3), he continues to bring about deception in the validity of God's word to heal. As the Church doubts, sickness and disease move in and overtake God's soldiers. As was seen in the rise of plagues that resulted in the deaths of thousands.

At this point, it seems necessary to interject a vital fact. Too many of God's soldiers are overly influenced by medical science. They claim that the sickness and disease is not spiritual but physical germs and bacteria. As if God doesn't know about germs or bacteria.

Let's understand that all these germs, etc. are part of the Fall. There was no such thing in the Garden of Eden. The main point is that Satan is the cause of sickness and disease as the book of Job proves which will be shown further on in this book. At present, we must concern ourselves with the fact that Jesus spoiled the principalities and powers controlled by Satan with His death and resurrection (Colossians 2:15). The power and authority that Satan had over mankind was abolished by Christ. Now, concerning God's soldiers, all things are put under His feet which is His Body (Ephesians 1:22–23). That means that ALL of Satan's power has been stripped away by Jesus who gave the power to His Body. In other words, God's soldiers have power and authority over whatever power the devil had. We now have the supremacy over sin, sickness, disease, and poverty like Adam had in the Garden before he gave it to Satan.

Let's understand something here. Yes, the disease or sickness may be a germ or bacteria, but that is all part of the physical realm. If you read my previous book about faith's journey, you saw that as Christians, we must separate the physical realm from the spiritual realm. Our power is not of the physical realm, it comes from God who resides in the spiritual realm. The spiritual or supernatural realm supersedes the physical or natural realm. Faith is part of the supernatural realm, for it is an attribute of God. Therefore, faith is greater than any physical germ or bacteria that is part of this natural realm. This will become more illuminated as we go on.

1. Bailey, *The Children's Bread*, 222.

The other point of note is that persecution, as revealed in chapter four, did not weaken but strengthen the Church. As war brings out the heroic qualities of men, so did the persecutions develop the patience, the gentleness, the endurance of Christians, and prove to the world conquering power of faith.[2] It appears that as one died, many rose in his place. This truth had been stated by Christ who said, " . . . except a corn of wheat fall into the ground and die, it abideth alone, but if it die, it bringeth forth much fruit" (John 12:24). Satan will not destroy (wear out) God's soldiers through persecution. Christ's Church does not weaken, but strengthen under the vilest of persecution. This fact must be comprehended in order to receive the revelation of this book about Daniel 7:25 and Satan's strategic plot to torment believers by inflicting sickness and disease.

Cyclic Pattern of Divine Healing Reveals the Deterioration of the Doctrine to be the Prerequisite for Satanic Attack

The diseases of Egypt represent a bitterness which besets man's lot in life. Howbeit, God's soldiers were to be distinguished. They were to be set apart from the Egyptians or the world (Exodus 8:22–23). Christ's atoning work on Calvary confirms God's covenant of healing. On the cross, the Christian has been provided with spiritual and physical healing (Matthew 8:16–17; Isaiah 53:4–5). Jesus has borne all our sicknesses, as well as all our sins.

Jesus healed extensively and made it part of the Christian mission of deliverance. In His Name is assurance that demons will be cast out and healing will be the result of laying on of hands (Mark 16:15–18). Yet, the power to believe and practice healing has almost slipped back into the Dark Age mentality of unbelief. As soon as we pray "if it is God's will" we have revealed our lack of faith in Divine Healing. Or if the person is not healed, we can attribute our lack of faith or their lack of faith as being God's will to

2. Schaff, *History of the Christian Church*, 33, Volume 2.

not heal. Unless, God is calling us home, or it is a sickness in which His glory is to be witnessed, it is His will for us to be in health. Scripture attests to this truth (2 Timothy 4:6; John 11:4).

As seen through the brief examination of the history of the Church and its practice of Divine Healing, it was disclosed that the belief of the Apostolic fathers concerning healing was at a peak for about the first eight centuries. After that time, the Church backed away from earnestly contending for the faith which was once and for all delivered to them. Faith healing was substituted by man into a sacrament of unbelief. It was no longer anointing the sick to recover, but anointing the sick to die. How far from the truth of Scripture the Church had fallen. Yet, even today, many of God's soldiers are still accepting sickness and disease as the will of God and are bowing down to the devil's lies. If that malady (a thorn in the flesh) does not reveal the power of God in a mighty way, we are to be healed. Anything that prohibits us from performing the call of God on our life is an attack of Satan. The only time we won't be healed is if we are being called home through this sickness. The Church must once again rise up in the full armor of God, wield the sword of the Spirit, cut to pieces his lies, and defeat Satan.

Faith in Divine Healing seems to be a doctrine that is believed but not readily practiced in the Church. Some Pentecostal and Charismatic circles, who were the staunch defenders, are sinking into doubt with so few actual healings. God warns in 1 Corinthians 15:33 that evil communications will corrupt right living. When I read many commentaries that are widely read and accepted by God's soldiers, many claimed that the Atonement (Christ's expiating sacrifice) cured the diseases of the soul. When physical healing is mentioned, most declared that it was not included in the Atonement.

One of the most influential works in the Pentecostal and Charismatic Churches is the New International Version Study Bible. Kenneth Barker gives the following comment on 1 Peter 2:24:

> "Not generally viewed as a reference to physical healing, though some believe that such healing was included in the Atonement (c.f. Matthew 8:16–17). Others see

spiritual healing in this passage. It is another way of as-
serting that Christ's death brings salvation to those who
trust in him."[3]

Apparently, the initiators responsible for this Bible seem to treat
neutrality as safe ground. However, the Greek word for healed in 1
Peter 2:24 means to heal or make whole. It is talking about making
us whole or a complete restoration spiritually, physically, emo-
tionally, and in every way that we need. Jesus didn't only heal the
people spiritually when here, but He was concerned about their
physical well-being. As this book will reveal, sickness and disease
left to run rampant in God's soldiers will hinder their spiritual
walk. Christ claims that lukewarm attitudes make Him sick (Revelation 3:15–16). God wants the Church to have a definitive stance
(be hot or cold). Such neutrality as found in many commentaries
could cause the faith of God's soldiers to believe God for healing
to waiver. Doubt will lead to unbelief. When God's soldiers doubt,
we are double minded and unstable like a wave of the sea driven
with the wind and tossed. We will not receive anything from the
Lord (James 1:6–8).

The father of lies (John 8:44) has placed the bait of doubting God's word as he did with Eve (Genesis 3:1). To question the
validity of the Scriptures puts us on unstable ground and we are
no longer standing on solid ground. The subtle and gradual acceptance of sickness has crept in unawares from of old. Ignorance
and misunderstanding have caused many in the Body of Christ to
accept erroneous teachings about Divine Healing. Where faith in
the word of God once reigned in the Early Church, it was replaced
by doubt in God's word. Why else would a doctrine of anointing
the sick to recover be replaced by a sacrament to anoint the sick to
die? Think about that. We must pray for God to enlighten the eyes
of His soldiers to see that faith in His ability to heal the sick was
turned into a sacrament to anoint someone for death.

The reappearance or reviving of faith healing about the six-
teenth century started to shatter the devil's lies, and proved that

---

3. Barker, *The NIV Study Bible*, 2389.

Jehovah-Rapha had not changed. Man had changed God through unbelief. Again, the Church rose up and stood against the wiles of the devil to defeat sickness and disease as she had been commissioned by Christ.

By the time of the end of the eighteenth century, the Reformers drove home that the Early Church had power because they believed. They had faith in God's word. Healing was expected, and God delivered. The Lord watches for opportunities to show Himself strong on behalf of those who will believe (2 Chronicles 16:9). Because they held God to His promise (they believed without waiver), He was able to keep His healing covenant as declared in Exodus 15:26.

During the beginning of the twentieth century, the deterioration began again. Satan put out his enticement a little different this time, but, of course, with the same end in view. Instead of attacking the doctrine of Divine Healing directly, he brought attention to the practices among the Pentecostals that were called fanatical. Much opposition from mainline denominations caused many in the Church to reject their methods. Some insisted that the Spirit filled believers were cultic. Sounds like the "so-called" religious group of our Lord's day once again infiltrated the Church to bring about doubt in Christ's work. To reject healing because of the Pentecostals was falling right into the hands of devil's lies.

It appears that the bottom line for the negative verbalism was to cause doubt in God's work as to whether or not the Pentecostal experience was for today. A fear of being recognized as belonging to the fanatics caused many believers to rescind in faith healing. Since the fanatical Pentecostals accepted and practiced Divine Healing, the fearful and unbelieving let their practice of Divine Healing fall by the wayside. Thus, many that could have been healed were left diseased and inform. However, it seems the widespread influence of unbelief, has now found itself in both the Pentecostal and Charismatic camps. A little leaven will eventually corrupt the whole (Galatians 5:9).

Let's expound and expand what has been said in this section and weigh the facts. In the garden, Eve believed God. She walked in the fullness of His blessings, until the day that she allowed the devil to deceive her into doubting God's word. Satan lied and she took his words as truth. Once Adam decided to follow suit and partake of the forbidden fruit, their blissful state ended. Man paid the consequences of unbelief. He not only became a sinner, but the physical body, once immune to infirmity, now experienced sickness and disease. Thus, opening the door for the devil to "wear out" God's people through physical infirmity.

Time goes by with God's people suffering sickness and disease without any protest against Satan. Then, the Early Church is enlightened through Christ that God desires to bless His people spiritually and physically. He has given us authority over Satan and all his power. As Satan and sin brought sickness and disease, Christ's Atonement brought spiritual and physical health. In other words, faith in Christ reverses the repercussions of the Fall. All that was lost in Adam has been regained through Christ. The only enemy yet to be put under is death (1 Corinthians 15:26), NOT SICKNESS AND DISEASE.

The Early Church held firmly onto the truth that, through Christ, believers have authority over Satan's power. This truth remained until the devil put in a wedge of unbelief. God's people wavered from anointing and expecting health, to anointing and expecting death. Again, (as in the garden) is revealed that before Satan begins to "wear out" the saints through sickness and disease, ignorance and unbelief in God's word come first.

This went on for centuries until the Reformers grasped hold of faith in God. As faith escalated, God's soldiers rose again to the heights of faith that God had intended. The God that said He was "Healer" was believed to be such. Satan could no longer get away with holding captive the Church through sickness and disease. Faith broke the bonds and believers were set free. God, once again, had His rightful place as Jehovah-Rapha, the Lord that heals. God's soldiers joined Him in His covenant of healing. However, Satan was determined to destroy the Church (he is the thief that steals, kills, and destroys, John 10:10). Once again, he crept in and brought about doubt and unbelief until those advocating Divine Healing questioned the doctrine.

Every time Satan put out his seed of doubt, God's soldiers have swallowed it hook, line, and sinker. Only to drown in the depths of unbelief, followed by sickness and disease. This fact has already been traced in chapter three to the Fall where sin opened the door to sickness and disease. Man was lured by Satan's lies and treacherous methods against God and His word. Instead of listening to God who makes clear that we are to give no place to the devil (Ephesians 4:27), God's soldiers listened to the devils lies. As mankind listened to Satan, he began to doubt God. In unbelief, we exchanged the truth for a lie. God's soldiers accepted the power of the devil (sin, sickness, and disease) and rejected the power of God (holiness and health).

The question that arises is what does all this amount to? Really, it is quite simple. The devil does not want the Church to be the head, but the tail. Sickness and disease tend to breed self-centeredness, because attention is devoted to the infliction. It is laborious to do battle when the physical body is overpowered with sickness and disease. Common sense clarifies this fact in the natural realm. A soldier who has been wounded by the enemy loses all sense of the battle. Once a dynamic warrior, now, the pain in his body has turned his thoughts to himself. This is precisely what has happened to many in the Church. Once great soldiers of God, now overcome by the sickness and disease in their body, the performance of lowly tasks is a hardship on them.

While working on this, the author took a serious look at some in the Church who are now overtaken by physical infirmity. Some incredible instances of past persecution by the enemy were revealed through the lives of these believers. Their previous warfare could have placed them among the heroes of faith listed in the book of Hebrews. One of these is a pastor who recalled that while backing out of his driveway, he ran over his young son. Through it all, his faith was kept strong, and he managed to perform his pastoral duties. Next, was a Church member whose wife had run away with the pastor of the church. Yet, he came out with a stronger faith than he went in with. Third, was a pastor who had been falsely accused by a Church member of sexual assault. His faith in God kept him going. He stood on God's promises and was vindicated. However, years later, all are now weary (worn out) due to physical infirmity. Before this, they were able to fight Satan and come through victoriously through his vicious attacks. Now, day after day, week after week, and year after year, the sickness in their body hinders them from fulfilling their work for the Lord.

God never intended for His saints to be ruled by the powers of Hell. It must be made clear that the devil's power include sickness and disease. God's soldiers are not to be dominated by any power from Hell (Luke 10:19). Nonetheless, many have succumbed through unbelief. Every time the enemy has gained a foothold on the people of God, it was through his efforts to bring about doubt in the legitimacy of God's Word. This tactic weakens the Church and makes the saints easy targets for destruction. It is this author's belief that nothing the enemy does, demilitarizes the Church as the torment of physical ailments. When our body is rebelling against us, we lose focus of the war with Satan and concentrate on our infirmity. In other words, the enemy has us under his control. We are no longer a threat to his kingdom, for we have become self-conscious.

The most convincing witness against the greatness of God is the soldier who sits as Job busying himself all day with his sickness and disease. Those observing him wonder what happened to his "healing" God, as they observe sickness and disease destroy (wear out) his faith. Instead of his life revealing that His God is all-powerful, he is divulging a god of impotence. Listen up, God's soldiers are not wearing the full armor of God and are being defeated by a conquered enemy. It's time to wake out of our slumber of accepting the devil's lies and stand against him as the more than conquerors that we are in Christ who loves us (Romans 8:37). To do this, we must be fully armed in the full armor of God.

I am not stating that sickness will not come, but that God's soldiers have authority over its effect to keep us down. Christ has given us power over the enemy. We are not the conquered. Jesus triumphed over all the demonic forces and satanic powers of the world through His death on the cross (Colossians 2:15). Satan was stripped of his power over God's soldiers to hold us captive to his dominion against our will. Through Christ, the Church now possesses the power to wage war against the spiritual forces of the devil. We do not have to remain captive to any satanic power (this is not only sin, but sickness and disease). Job remained captive, because he did not have the correct knowledge of God. I will not go into to detail about that as it is covered in my book, *Storms Are Faith's Workout: Preparing Christians for Spiritual Ambush.*

Job Reveals Persecution Does Not Weaken Faith

In all of Bible history, none is more acclaimed for his longsuffering or patience during persecution than Job (James 5:11). Any of God's soldiers who have read about his ordeal in the book of Job cannot deny him the number one status of those who have endured incredible satanic attack. If there had been an award for "persecution," Job would have been the recipient of the first.

Common knowledge teaches that Job reveals the suffering of the righteous does not equate punishment for sin. However, this book is not going to embark on any doctrinal debate on the book of Job. The purpose of this book is to establish enough evidence from the book of Job to ascertain the author's belief concerning the lack of Divine Healing in the Church. The interest in Job's persecution is only as it establishes the method in which Satan will "wear out the saints" in Daniel 7:25.

Since Satan is to wear out the saints of the Most High, it is essential that the character of Job be established. To accredit to him the title of "saint," he must have the credentials required. Scripture leaves no question in that aspect. He is called "perfect and upright, one that feared God, and eschewed evil" (Job 1:1). In verse eight, God Himself acclaims righteousness to Job. His moral integrity was one of rightness in word, thought, and action. Job was whole heartily committed to God. He is unquestionably considered a "saint" of God, by God's own confession of his righteousness.

Satan is introduced in Job as the accuser of the brethren. When confronted by God about Job's uprightness, his accusation against Job is that he serves God for His blessings. Unable to previously corrupt him, Satan claimed that the loss of temporal blessings would reveal Job's true character. God, while limiting Satan's power against His servant, accepted the challenge. Job was "given into his (Satan's) hand (Job 1:12).

Convinced that Job will curse God to His face, Satan began his diabolical attack. The troubles brought upon Job came all at once. One messenger was unable to finish his story before the next one arrived. Messenger after messenger reported the devastating news. First, he was told the Sabaeans slew his servants and stole his oxen and asses. Next, he is informed that a fire from heaven burned the sheep and consumed his servants. After that, it was reported that Chaldeans took his camels and slaughtered his servants. The last reported that a great wind had caused the death of his ten children.

Job was robbed of 500 yoke of oxen, and 500 she-asses, 7,000 sheep, 3,000 camels, his servants, and ten children. His dearest and most valuable possessions were his ten children who were killed and buried in the ruins. This was not only the greatest of his losses, but the most wounding. The devil left it for last, if the other provocations failed, this would cause Job to curse God. Thus, Satan did all that he desired against job, to provoke him to curse God. He touched all he had, leaving him a poor man.

Although Job reacted to the disasters that happened to him with intense grief, he humbled himself under the hand of God. In all this Job sinned not, nor charged God foolishly. The devil claimed that under such persecution, he would curse God. However, Job blessed Him (Job 1:20–21). He gave glory to God in the midst of extreme adversity.

At this point, it is important to stop and ponder the facts. The persecution that Job suffered was intense, to say the least. Yet, he remains unshaken in his faith and devotion to God. Satan did not "wear out" Job during intense persecution. Even in this time of darkness, being stripped of everything which men call dear, he fell down and worshipped God. He steadfastly held his devotion to God. The man did not waiver in his faith under extraordinary ruin.

The second chapter of Job opens with more or less the same dialogue as chapter one. Only this time, God points out to the devil that his scheme against Job did not work and that Job held fast his integrity. At this, Satan asserted that touching him *physically* would cause him to curse God. Again, Job was "given into his hand" (Job 2:6). The devil was persuaded that "skin for skin" is man's weakness (2:4). Satan was convinced that man's vulnerability is in his physical body. In verse five, he tells God to touch his bone. In other words, as Matthew Poole paraphrases this verse:

> "Smite him, not slightly, but to the quick, and to the bones and marrow, in order to make him feel pain and anguish."[4]

Satan was not looking to inflict Job with some small malady. The devil wanted Job to be incapacitated, in the sense that all he could do was focus on his physical infirmity. To feel pain and anguish is to experience agony, torment, distress, grief, anxiety, and misery. Satan was ingenious in inflicting pain upon Job. His infliction was a burning sore, an inflammation that covered his whole body. Job was in continuous misery with a sore too disgusting to touch; he had to use a potsherd (a piece of broken pottery) to scrape himself.

Job's wife proved to be the aggravation of his misery. Because of his apparent stench, she wanted nothing to do with him (Job 19:17). To make matters worse, she tempts him to curse God and accuses that his integrity brought him nowhere. She concludes that he might as well curse God, die, and end his torment. Job maintains his character and charges his wife with being an inconsiderate and weak person. He declared that it was only fitting to receive both good and evil from the Lord. In all this, Job did not sin with his lips (Job 2:9–10).

4. Poole, *Matthew Poole's Commentary on the Bible*, 925, Volume 1.

In the third chapter of Job, we find Job cursing the day of his birth. Here is where Job begins to weaken. He has been bereaved, disgraced, and persecuted. His greatest pain in all of this was his believing that God had done this to him and has left him. Although he did not make any direct accusations at God, he did make secret and indirect reflections against God's providence. He cast blame upon God for bringing the day of his birth about. In this, Job's curse was sinful.

The discourse between Job and his friend exposes their spiritual ignorance matched that of Job's. The ignorance of Job is revealed when he blamed God for his disasters. His friends displayed their lack of knowledge in believing that Job's circumstance was due to personal sin. Job accepted his sickness as being the hand of God. His friends accepted his sickness as being the hand of God for unrighteousness. Either way, it was the general consensus that God was creator of his physical infirmity. Believing that, made Job defenseless. That is exactly what the devil wants God's soldiers to believe today.

We must understand this important fact. If we accept something as coming from God, we feel helpless. How can we contend with God? When the devil has us in that place, he knows that we are pawns in his hands. Unless God's soldiers realize that sickness and disease originate from Satan, we will not take the authority over him that Jesus has given us. Like I stated earlier, germs and bacteria are part of this natural realm. This means that they don't exist in the spiritual realm where faith supersedes anything in this realm. That is why Jesus said that their faith had made them whole (Mark 5:34; Luke 17:19; Mark 10:52). Faith is greater than anything that is part of this natural realm, for it is part of the supernatural realm of God.

Let's continue with the story of Job. It is shown that Job begins to "wear out" more and more. In chapter sixteen, Job states, "He teareth me in His wrath." Job felt as if God was pursuing him with a deadly hatred. He believed that he was being treated like an enemy. He continues in his tormented state of believing that God has forsaken him. For in chapter twenty-three and verse three, he cries out in desperation, "Oh that I knew where I might find him! That I might come even to his seat."

Job was declaring that his desire was for the presence of God, but God was ignoring him. His heart was crying out to God from the depths of sorrow, but he felt that God had no heart of mercy for him. In chapter thirty, Job reflects this same mentality with, "I cry unto thee, and thou dost not hear me: I stand up, and thou regardest me not." Here, Job claims that he persists in prayer continually, but God shows no pity. He accuses God of finding pleasure in his suffering. Job actually blames God for his misery and declares that God has all the while enjoyed it.

When God addresses Job in chapter thirty-eight, He reveals Job's ignorance about the Divine role in all that was happening. God used Job's ignorance of the earth's natural order to reveal his ignorance of God's moral order. If Job did not understand the workings of God's physical creation, how could he possibly understand God's mind and character? As the revelation continues, chapter forty opens with Job humbling himself before God. He was overwhelmed by this new revelation of God and felt that he could say no more. Job learned that he had pointed his finger in the wrong direction. It was Satan and not God who was his enemy.

Job entered his trials as a blind man. He was without the revelational truths the Church has today in the Scriptures. God had never left him (Hebrews 13:5). However, Job did not have the book of Hebrews with which to know this. He did not have the book of Job to view the conversation between the accuser of the brethren and God, or the order of events the enemy chose to bring about his torment. He did not have Daniel 7:25 to warn him of Satan's plot to "wear out" the saints of God through sickness and disease. Furthermore, he did not have 2 Corinthians 2:11 to know that he did not have to be ignorant of Satan's devices. Job did not know that he had the authority over the devil's power to inflict sickness and disease (Luke 10:19). However, God's soldiers are supposed to know this. We have all the Scriptures and all the examples in the Bible that reveal that we are no longer under bondage to any of Satan's power. Christ has set the captive free. If the Son therefore shall make you free, ye shall be free indeed (John 8:36)!

6

Conclusion

THE EVIDENCE BROUGHT FORTH in this book clearly describes that Satan's most powerful tool against the Church is the infliction of any physical infirmity. It is unmistakably his prerequisite for "wearing out the saints." Chapter four revealed that he has used persecution of all types to demobilize the Church. Each time he watched her grow stronger and that martyrdom seemed to breed believers. As stated in chapter three, Christ had forewarned His disciples that "if they persecuted me, they will persecute you" (John 15:20). This became an incredible reality all too soon, with God's soldiers being tempered in the fires of persecution.

Chapter four exposed that, at first, Church persecution was mainly local, sporadic, and more often the result of mob action rather than the result of definite civil policy. After 250 A.D., however, persecution became, at times, the studied strategy of the Roman imperial government that was widespread and violent. During that time Tertullian's idea that "the blood of Christians is seed" (of the Church) became a terrible reality to many Christians.[1] It was a determined and systematic attempt to uproot Christianity completely and wipe the Church off the face of the earth. Christian torture was made sport in the arena. Many Christians were crucified. Some were sewed up in the skins of the wild beasts. Then big

1. Cairns, *Christianity Through the Centuries*, 87.

dogs were let loose upon them and they were torn to pieces. Others were beheaded, burned at the stake, etc. Every torture imagined by man was used against God's soldiers to exterminate the Church. However, it only bred believers like plants in a conservatory.

During the Reformation, martyrs such as William Tyndale, John Hus, Michael Sattler, etc. proved that the Church will not be stopped under the severest of persecution. Their testimonies are incredible. I mean how fantastic is it to sing while being burned at the stake. Their testimonies reveal the most striking strength of God's grace. Truly His grace is sufficient, for His strength is made perfect in weakness.

Since chapter four covered sufficiently the subject of Church persecution, it is not necessary to go on with much detail about persecution. In summary, there were long subjugation and a constant course of hardships put upon God's soldiers, ruining their estates, weakening their families, and martyrdom. All of which did not wear down or wear out the Church.

When discussing the mental anguish of the afflicted in chapter four, it was seen that they had endured persecution, hardships, torture, losses, etc. It is only continual sickness and disease in their bodies that wears out the saints, as revealed in chapter five. With careful consideration of the language given concerning "wear out" along with the information collected through researching past persecution of the Church, it is revealed that Satan must use more decisive methods to wear down (wear out) the saints of God than has been the general consensus.

In the analysis of Job, it was evidenced that he had endured losses, and did not foolishly charge God. Yes, Job reacted to the disasters that happened to him with intense grief, but in no way was worn down by the enemy's plot against him (Job 1). Even when Job was first stricken with physical illness, he did not waiver. As a matter of fact, he rebuked his foolish wife (Job 2). Job began to wear down (suffer mental affliction) only as his illness remained day after day. This is revealed in his cursing the day he was born (Job 3).

Throughout the Christian world, many have suffered severe persecution and martyrdom. To believe that such things are a part of history and not of today is to be regretfully misinformed. A thing of the past is not the case in some areas of the world. Many in America do not realize that Christians in other countries are suffering daily for their faith in Christ. According to David Barrett of the World Evangelization Research Center:

> "Martyrdom is a regular, ongoing feature of Church life in 25 percent of global Christianity that we call the "underground church." In one part of the globe, over ten thousand Christians have been killed every year since 1950, due to clashes with anti-Christian mobs, infuriated relatives, state-organized death squads, and so on."[2]

In order for that many to be martyred, the Church must be growing at incredible rates. If persecution is supposed to wear out the saints, as believed to be the interpretation of Daniel 7:25, why is the Church growing so rapidly under phenomenal persecution?

Ignorance Attributes Sickness to the Will of God

Job's ignorance and lack of spiritual knowledge is understandable. God, however, will not wink at ignorance in His saints today. To sit and scrape one's sore with a potsherd is to give sickness which is the power of Satan the authority that he does not have. Satan has taken advantage of the Church's ignorance and unbelief to keep believers from being healed.

This author is not claiming that sickness will not come at us nor that we won't go under its power. I believe that it is to test our faith in who has the authority. Is it the lying devil or God's soldiers? When I was in a battle with ulcerated colitis, I was hospitalized. It was so severe, the pills that they gave me came out just as whole as they were when they went in. Anyway, when I asked the doctor if there was any cure, he said there was none. When the words came

2. Reapsome, *Christian History Magazine*, 37, Issue 27, Volume IX, Number 3.

out of his mouth, I heard in my spirit, "That's a lie. I am He that healeth thee. Trust Me. I will lead you. Your body was created to heal itself. Follow My instructions and I will heal you." Of course, I expected to be healed immediately. However, I had a road to travel to gain knowledge and wisdom. It took time to research for natural supplements. But after being faithful to what the Lord led me to take, I gradually was able to eat what I could not eat before without a bout. It has been seven years that I have been able to eat anything. I still take the natural supplements that He led me to take, and I feel completely normal.

What I am trying to reveal here is that if I had listened to the doctor, I would have stayed on the prescriptions that would have caused all kinds of adverse reactions. Doing so, I would still have ulcerated colitis and whatever the prescriptions would have caused. When I read what they caused, I cried out to the Lord to please protect me while I followed His leading to the natural supplements. Within a couple of months, I was off all but one of the prescriptions. I stayed on it until the diarrhea was under control. But within about six months, I was able to stop that one. For about a year after, I had to make sure that I didn't eat anything that would trigger a bout. Natural supplements take longer to work because they don't just cover up the symptoms, they heal the root or cause of the problem.

Jesus is not the one who steals, kills, and destroys. Satan is the thief and destroyer of men. Jesus is the Giver of the abundant life. Dominion of satanic power is broken. Christ gave His Church power (authority) over all the powers of Hell. Just as sin is a fleshly weakness, so is sickness. The flesh must yield to sin, and it must yield to sickness. That may seem difficult for some to comprehend, but sin and sickness are of the natural realm. Righteousness and health are of the supernatural realm. There is no sin, sickness, or disease in Heaven. As God's soldiers, we must remember that we are seated in heavenly places with Christ which is far above all principalities, powers, sin, sickness, etc. That's why we must realize that faith is not of this physical realm, but of the spiritual realm of God. Faith is a supernatural power of God. As we believe Him,

He does what is impossible in this realm when we believe Him to do it.

Let me explain what I mean by yielding to its power. Our flesh is weak and as the power of sin is strong so is the power of sickness. If we don't take authority over the power of sin, it will overpower us in its grip. We must realize that as we have power over sin in Christ's Atonement, we have authority over sickness and disease in His Atonement. If we don't take authority over sickness, it will also overpower us in its grip. What we must realize is that God's soldiers will wrestle the dominion from demonic powers and continue in warfare against the arch enemy of the cross until Christ returns. That means that we have the power and we must not allow the devil to convince us otherwise. Yes, it is difficult when the devil ambushes us with his lies and our foundation is shook. But as soon as he sends his lies, we must do as Christ did and counter his lies with truth of God's word. We must study the Scriptures and become fluent with the sword of the Spirit. Thus, when the devil throws his diabolical obstacles in our path, we will cut to pieces his lies and deceit. The armor of God is discussed at length in my book, *Faith's Journey Confronts Obstacles: Instructing God's Soldiers to Overcome in His Armor*.

Those lacking Biblical revelation (knowledge of the Scriptures) will make reference to Job in their dispute that sickness is God's will for many people. God's permitting Satan to inflict him was to display Job's steadfastness in the face of adversity. The main point, however, is not God's permission, Job's infirmity, or faithfulness, it is that the affliction was the direct work of the devil. God was not the author of Job's sickness. Sickness was the strategy of Satan who desired to shatter Job's faith in God. That is precisely what the devil is trying to do to many in the Church today. As I stated earlier, I do believe that some may have a thorn in their flesh. However, it will not prohibit or limit them in doing what God has called them to do. If it hinders the work of the Lord, then it is not a thorn allowed by the Lord. It is a satanic maneuver to obstruct God's will in the life.

It is this author's belief that sometimes a thorn in flesh is allowed by God to demonstrate that His grace is sufficient. In spite of the thorn, the person is enabled to do extraordinary things for the Lord that people without a thorn are amazed at the power of God working in the person. I remember a young man that was in an accident and lost a leg. He had been raised in the Church, but went wild and joined in with the wrong crowd. A drunken party ended in a car wreck and the loss of his leg. The young man became a powerful tool for the Lord. He told the other youth in the Church not to feel sorry for him, for it was better to enter Heaven with one leg than to enter Hell with both of them.

As we look at Job, we see that as he grew in knowledge and understanding of the Divine, he felt shame and repented of his belief that God caused his calamities. He was embarrassed at accusing the Almighty of not hearing his cries, and leaving him pitiless. Job had no way of previously knowing what God had revealed to him. With his new found knowledge, Job was restored to health.

Each of God's soldiers are conscience of the progress or growth that takes place in our knowledge of the Scriptures. When we were a child, we could only think as a child. We could not grasp the truths of adulthood until we became mature. However, that did not mean that all the facts, truths, doctrines, and principles dealing with Christian theology, were not in the Bible. Since our food has gone from milk to strong meat, we digest what could not be digested before. There have been no additions made to the Scriptures we fed upon as a young Christian. It is that our spiritual eyes have matured to clearly see what we previously saw vaguely. The maturity in God's soldiers theological knowledge was affected by a continual and gradual process as a child goes from adolescence to adulthood. It is as stated in my first book, *Storms Are Faith's Workout: Preparing Christians for Spiritual Ambush*. A first grader can only be tested with a first grade test. Then move on to second grade, etc. It is the same way in our Christian walk, we go from faith to faith. As we pass first grade, so to speak, we go to second grade, and so forth. Each time, our knowledge of God and faith in His ability increases.

This author comprehends the necessity for faith to increase. In *Storms Are Faith's Workout*, I revealed my battle to overcome a neck injury that had me bedridden. In *Faith's Journey Confronts Obstacles*, I spoke about the ulcerated colitis. This book reveals more of my battle to overcome ulcerated colitis. There were times that the Lord healed me after the laying on of hands and prayer. However, if I had not battled my flesh in the times that I had to obey and take supplements, I would have never learned that God created our bodies to heal themselves when proper nutrients are taken.

Furthermore, it illuminated that as we must fight our flesh against sin, we must battle our flesh against sickness and disease. Sin is always lying at the door to overtake us, and sickness and disease are always trying to overtake us. Our flesh is weak and if we yield to its weakness, we will sin, and we will become sick. But if we yield to the Spirit, we will overcome any sin and any sickness. We may have to wrestle our flesh in agony, but we will come away victoriously. The only time that we will not be enabled to overcome the physical malady is when death is about to have its way. If we are in a right relationship with the Lord, He will let us know that this is the sickness that will take us home.

God's Soldiers Are Not to be Ignorant of Satan's Devices

Because the truth of the Bible are not systematically stated, but scattered throughout, it is necessary to search and search to discover the treasures (truths) to be had. A research of the word of God reveals there is more available that has yet to be learned or comprehended. However, it is sin to sit in ignorance like Job. God has revealed His character through His written word which Job did not have.

Why do God's soldiers so readily accept the torment from Satan against our physical body and at the same time claim to have power over him? When tried with sin, God's soldiers will quote that Christ has set us free, and that we have power or authority over Satan's power. Power or authority over Satan's power means power and authority over ALL his power. That means power over sickness and disease. Are not sickness and disease part of Satan's power? Then who has power over them? All of God's soldiers have been given that authority by Jesus who has rendered the devil powerless against His Church.

According to Daniel 7:25 and Job 2:6, God has placed God's soldiers in the hands of Satan to be inflicted with physical sickness and disease. He may have permission, but the Church has been given authority over anything and everything the devil may try to do. Christ (judgment) has sat, and God's soldiers are to take away Satan's dominion (Daniel 7:26). This is where we have to understand that after Christ's resurrection, He spoiled principalities and powers, made a show of them openly, and triumphed over them in it (Colossians 2:15). That means that Christ triumphed over all the satanic powers and demonic forces of this world. The devil has been stripped of his power to hold God's soldiers captive against our will. Because of Christ's conquest, Christians have victory over the world and temptation. We have been given the power to wage a victorious war against the spiritual forces of Hell (Ephesians 6:10–18).

Yes, this Scripture in Daniel is suggesting the future Millennium, however, the Bible is full of double references. The law of double reference in Scripture means that it holds multiple meanings. For example, Ezekiel 28:11–19 speaks about the king of Tyrus while at the same time referring to Satan. With that in mind, it is wise to remember that Jesus gave us authority over all the power of Satan. It is not a future reality, but a present fact (Luke 10:19). God's soldiers who give dominance of self (through sin or sickness) to the devil is doing so against the will of God. In other words, it is God's will that the whole man be healed. As sin is not His will for us, neither is sickness or disease. We must comprehend that the only enemy that is not put under God's soldiers authority is death (1 Corinthians 15:26).

In order to possess the kingdom, God's soldiers must continuously advance and conquer the territory Satan has robbed from us through his lying and deceiving tactics. Granted, the Church lost much territory in the first Adam who literally handed all things over to Satan. Howbeit, it did not stay in his hands. The second Adam (Christ) conquered the strongholds of Hell and "God has put ALL THINGS under His feet, who has been made the Head to the Church" (Ephesians 1:22). We are His Body and ALL things are under His feet. If we are His Body, that means ALL things are under our feet. In other words, the devil's power is under our feet. God's soldiers must stop allowing Satan's lies to nurture unbelief in us. It is time for us to stand against his lies in the full armor of God and be unwavering in our faith.

Christ told the Christian to "Occupy till I come" (Luke 19:13). What is the Christian to occupy or hold on to? What else, but the kingdom (the territory, the truths, dominion of himself/herself) that God has given us who are born again. In order to hold on to what we have received, communicates or reveals a process that involves a long struggle requiring God's soldiers to be steadfast, unmovable, always abounding in the work of the Lord (1 Corinthians 15:58). God accomplished the foundational victory at the cross, and through the cross is the decisive victory that allows us to go in (do battle against the forces of Hell) and possess that which God has promised.

Knowledge is the Determinate Factor in Recognizing Satan's Scheme

In the Atonement, God took care of all that which the Fall had bestowed upon man. This includes physical and spiritual salvation (deliverance). Man was healed (the cross is past tense) by Christ's stripes (Isaiah 53:5; I Peter 2:24). Yet, the father of lies encourages unbelief in the efficacy of the Atonement. The devil knows that if God's soldiers do not have faith in the complete work included in the Atonement, he can (and will) "wear out" all who fall prey to his diabolical scheme. Dr. Hamon of Christian International School describes Satan's fiendish design like this:

> "Jesus took away all power of the devil and delivered it unto the Church. The devil refuses to acknowledge that he is defeated or to relinquish his dominion of this

world to the Church. He has maintained his position, and restrained the Church by keeping it blinded to its rightful position. HE CONTINUALLY CONVINCES THE CHURCH THAT GOD'S WORD DOESN'T RE-ALLY MEAN WHAT IT SAYS: that the Church cannot do all that Christ Jesus says we can do and that we don't really have what God's Word declares we have. As long as Satan can find professing preachers and teachers of Christianity who will work with him, he can keep the Church bound and restricted by doctrines of devils and man-made creeds. The devil knows that the Church has "power over all the power of the enemy" and "all things are possible" if the Church would only believe."[3]

Satan plans to literally "wear out" God's people through sickness and disease as described in Daniel 7:25. Yes, there will always be persecution in many forms in this life, but none has proven to discourage the saints like bodily sickness and disease. Job, as well as the previously mentioned who were martyred, gives unquestionable evidence that the Church can withstand great temporal losses. God's soldiers grow weary ("wear out") when bodily infirmity continues to persist. We seem to be able to fight and fight the enemy to overcome sin, to pray through, etc. But when God's soldiers are physically debilitated, we give into man's knowledge and turn to drugs that cause side effects many times worse than the sickness or disease the drugs were taken for. This is not to say that medical science cannot help at times, but to put faith in men instead of God means that Divine Healing is eliminated. We become addicted to whatever prescription the doctor prescribes because the drugs cannot heal the body. They only cover up the symptoms of the sickness or disease that are getting worse as time goes by. Like stated earlier, I was on the prescriptions only as long it took for God to lead me to the supplements that would enable my body to heal itself.

A view of Church history recounts that false views, false inferences, misapprehensions, ignoring of some facts, and misinterpretations have come and gone in endless succession. Nevertheless,

3. Hamon, *The Eternal Church*, 145.

those with teachable spirits inevitably emerge as the overcomers. God will have a victorious Church that will not succumb to doubt and fear. In each generation, God will raise up those who will dare to believe Him and go against the tide of unbelief.

Jesus said, "These signs shall follow them that believe; In my name they shall cast out devils; they shall speak with new tongues . . . THEY SHALL LAY HANDS ON THE SICK, AND THEY SHALL RECOVER" (Mark 16:17–18).

In the historical synopsis of Divine Healing in chapter three, it was revealed that the signs promised by Jesus appear to those who believe. On the other hand, those who insist on doubting, can be sure the signs will be absent in their life. This is called faith in reverse. Faith determines what we receive. Matthew 9:29 says, "According to your faith be it unto you."

It is a matter of our learning that as we fight sin, we must fight sickness and disease. The flesh and the Spirit are contrary to each other. Our flesh will always fight the Spirit and God's will (Galatians 5:17). As Jacob wrestled all night, we must continuously wrestle against our flesh that wants to yield to sin and sickness (Genesis 32:24).

When Jesus was here, He made clear that He was concerned with our spiritual well-being and our physical well-being. In His concern for their spiritual health, He taught that the religious leaders were more concerned with teaching the doctrines of men (Matthew 15:9). Jesus warned that the leaven or teaching of the Pharisees and of the Sadducees that taught the traditions of men nullify the word of God (Matthew 16:6). Their teaching would not lead to God but to men. In His concern for their physical health, He is found healing the woman with the issue of blood (Luke 8:43–48). He raises the ruler of the synagogue's daughter from death (Mark 5:22–43). Ten lepers are healed (Luke 17:12–19).

Jesus heals not only spiritually but physically. God's soldiers must comprehend this truth and take the authority that has been given them over Satan. When we invoke the Name of Jesus, that is the Name that is above ALL names (Philippians 2:9–11). Do we understand that no matter how many names we name that they are ALL under Jesus. Any sin, any sickness, any disease, any malady is UNDER the NAME of JESUS. To further back that up, we are seated in Heavenly places with Christ Jesus (Ephesians 2:6). We are up there with Jesus above all that this world consists of. That's why we must understand that faith is not of this realm, it receives its power from the spiritual realm where God resides. Our faith is not rooted in our ability. Faith is rooted in God's faith to do what He says He will do. There isn't anything that God can't do (Luke 1:37). If God's soldiers would just understand that God created everything out of His faith (Hebrews 11:3), we would no longer doubt that He is Jehovah-Rapha, the Lord our Healer.

I am convinced that the evidence brought forth in this book has done one of two things. The first thing that this book has done is to convince God's soldiers who are unteachable to continue to believe the father of lies. These will continue to feed the ignorance of many and keep them bound to their sickbed wallowing in self-pity believing that God has forsaken them or that their sickness is God's will. Like I stated earlier, I do believe that there can be a thorn in the flesh that could be some sort of physical infirmity. However, it will exhibit the grace of God in a mighty way in that life. A thorn will not prohibit us from doing whatever God wills for our life. If we are incapacitated and unable to do what God has called us to do, we have been seduced into accepting the devil's lies.

The second is to be convinced that Daniel 7:25 refers to the onslaught of sickness and disease in God's soldiers. These will endeavor to enlighten others of Satan's strategy to mentally afflict or "wear out" the saints of God through sickness and disease. They will be like town criers to wake up God's soldiers to Satan's wicked plot and remind them that it is us who have the power over all the power of the enemy. Satan's power and authority was taken from him. After the Resurrection, Christ gave it to His disciples who are all of us that are born again. Sin, sickness, and disease have been conquered by Christ who gave the authority to God's soldiers. To put it plainly, Jesus took away the devil's power and authority over sin, sickness, and disease and gave it to YOU!

Bibliography

Bailey, Keith M., *Divine Healing: The Children's Bread*. Penn: Christian Publications Inc., 1997.

Barker, Kenneth, gen. ed., *NIV Study Bible*. Mich: Zondervan, 1985.

Barnes, Albert, *Barnes' Notes*. 14 vols., Mich: Baker House, 1983.

Bartleman, Frank, *Azusa Street*. New Jersey: Logos International, 1980.

Cairns, Earle E., *Christianity Through the Centuries*. Mich: Zondervan, 1977.

Clark, Adam, *Clark's Commentary*. 3 vols., Nashville: Abingdon, 1977.

Collins, Gary R., *Christian Counseling*. Texas: Word, 1988.

Dake, Finis Jennings, *Dake's Annotated Bible*. Georgia, Dake Bible Sales, Inc., 1987, KJV.

Foxe, John, *Foxe's Book of Martyrs*, New Jersey: Fleming H. Revell Company, 1965.

Frend, William H. C., *"Persecution in the Early Church,"* *Christian History*, Issue 27, 1990.

Gateway Films, *God's Outlaw—The Story of William Tyndale*. Penn: Vision Video Inc., 2030 Wentz Church Road, Worcester, 19490, 93 minutes.

———. *John Hus*. 55 minutes.

———. *The Radicals*. 99 minutes.

———. *The Trial and Testimony of the Early Church—From Christ to Constantine*. Penn: Vision Video Christian History Institute. Approximately 3 hours.

Hamon, Bill Dr., *The Eternal Church*. Florida: Christian International, 1981.

Hayford, Jack W., ed., *Spirit Filled Life Bible*. Mass: Hendrickson, 1991, NKJV.

Hillerbrand, Hans J., ed., *The Reformation*. Michigan: Baker House, 1992.

Hinn, Benny, *The Anointing*. Tenn: Thomas Nelson, 1992.

J. E. H. Thompson, *Exposition, The Pulpit Commentary*. Mass: Hendrickson, 23 vols, 1995.

Kuiper, B. D., *The Church in History*. Mich: Wm. B. Eerdmans, 1960.

Latourette, Kenneth Scott, *A History of Christianity*. California: Harper Collins, vol. 1, 1975.

McMillen, S. I., *None of These Diseases*. New Jersey: Fleming H. Revell Company, 1984.

Newman, Albert Henry, *A Manual of Church History*. 2 vols., Penn: The American Baptist Publication Society, 1949.

Pamphilus, Eusebius, *Ecclesiastical History*. Mich: Baker House, 1993.

Poole, Matthew, *Matthew Poole's Commentary*. 3 vols., Mass: Hendrickson, 1985.

Reapsome, James, "*Persecuted Christians Today,*" *Christian History*. Issue 27, vol IX, No. 3, 37.

Schaff, Philip, *History of the Christian Church*. 8 vols., Mich: Wm. B. Eerdmans, 1994.

Sheldon, Henry C., *History of the Christian Church*. 5 vols., Mass: Hendrickson, 1994.

Simpson, A. B., *The Gospel of Healing*. Penn: Christian Publications, 1986.

Smith, James, *Handfuls on Purpose*. 5 vols., Michigan: Wm. B. Eerdmans, 1993.

Stamps, Donald C., *The Fire Bible*. Mass: Hendrickson, 2017, KJV.

———. *The Full Life Study Bible*. Mich: Zondervan, 1992, KJV.

Strong, James, *The New Strong's Exhaustive concordance of the Bible*. Tenn: Thomas Nelson, 1990.

Vine, W. E.; Unger, Merrill F.; and William White, eds., *Vine's Complete Expository Dictionary of Old and New Testament Words*. Tenn: Thomas Nelson, 1985.

Webster, Noah, *1828, American Dictionary of the English Language*. California: Foundation for American Christian Education, 1993.